Copyright © 2019 by Skyler Chauff.

All rights reserved. This book or any portion thereof may not be reproduced or used in any manner whatsoever without the expressed written permission of the publisher except for the use of brief quotations in a book review.

Self-published, 2019.

3rd Edition.

Photo courtesy of St. John's Northwestern Military Academy.

CONTENTS

Copyright
Introduction-"You Did what?!"
One-Scoping Out Your Journey — 1
Two-911, What Is Your Emergency? — 7
Three-A Parent's Perspective: He Said, She Said — 16
Four-D-Day — 30
Five-Baby Steps — 44
Six-Breakthrough — 67
Seven-Nobody Cares About You, Forget Your Ego — 89
Eight-Be Like A Child — 97
Nine-Where "Self" Ends Up — 114
Ten-Finding One's Calling — 134
Eleven-Adolf Chauff, Yes Mr. Correctional Officer — 138
Twelve-It's the Journey, Not the Destination — 148
Thirteen-The Meaning in Relationships — 160
Fourteen-Balance — 169
Fifteen-This Is Their Story, This Is Their Path — 174
Acknowledgements — 176

INTRODUCTION- "YOU DID WHAT?!"

"So what'd you do to end up at a military school?" my friend's mom intrusively asked. Nice to meet you too, I thought. I found myself stuttering through my response, looking to avoid further interrogation. "I went for the academics," I replied. That was the same essential response I had provided my friends, family, and former teachers. There was more to why I left my friends, parents, and the sheltered public school environment, which had nurtured me since kindergarten. There was more to why I was accepting a military structure, a buzz cut haircut, a 6:30 a.m. wake up, and my favorite - outside accountability formations.

I had grown in so many different ways after just three months at St. John's Northwestern Military Academy. For starters, I was more mature, and I felt mentally, physically, and emotionally stronger. I now stood up straighter, spoke in a formal language that included 'Sir' and 'Ma'am,' and made my bed.

"Actually, Skyler was caught selling cocaine in 6th grade," my friend blurted.

As the mom's facial muscles twitched and her eyes bulged, I could feel my jaw clenching. Her blue eyes remained locked on mine as if I was some criminal - Al Capone, out to introduce her son to the nightlife of bar hopping and to christen him with shots of hard liquor. I spoke, my voice shaking with anger.

"That's not true, ma'am. He's joking."

"What's it like at..." she flared her nose again, "military school?"

I had rehearsed this one before. "It's different, it's challenging, but I love it. I've definitely matured a lot."

It didn't matter what I said. My friend's mother had already determined that her son would have to steer clear of my "bad influence."

The negative stigma around military school disappoints me. Military school "cadets" are some of the most organized high-schoolers in the United States. With a discipline foreign to the average student, these cadets are well-versed in leadership, time-management, conflict resolution, and goal-setting: skills necessary in the real world. Living independent of parental guidance, cadets are at a tremendous advantage as opposed to the average at-home student in the United States. Their learning extends far beyond the classroom.

A significant focus of this book is showing that military schools are not institutions for troubled youth. They are not juvenile reformatories for drug dealers, high-school dropouts, or delinquents. In my four years at military school, I've seen changed life after changed life, success story after success story. I am about to confront the negative stigma. This is my story - it inspired this book. As I wrote this book, starting my sophomore year, I couldn't stray from including some of the lessons I've learned. I want you to know precisely how an introverted, self-centered, and prideful human being like myself was able to learn from his mistakes and conquer them - and exactly how military school helped with that process.

Feel free to skip past my personal story if you are simply seeking direction on a particular aspect of your life. Perhaps you'll peruse the table of contents or choose a funny-sounding chapter and glean something of substance from it. Whether you read straight through or you stumble upon some random section, I hope that my accounts, blunders, and revelations throughout my journey help to enrich your life. Again, this book is meant to be more about you than me. I'll tell you right now; **I am not what you might think.** I'm not some superhuman robot machine. I'm not this unique amazing success story. My story is a series of slip-ups and a sequence of awkward moments, less than ideal decisions, missed opportunities, and much, much more. It just so happens that I believe my errors and the errors of others I mention could enrich your life, fix your mentality, and just possibly, change your world.

One might conclude that this is a Cinderella story, but I say this story is a string of mistakes, mishaps, and revelations - experiences no doubt that will make for an interesting read. Before I reveal my journey to you, I want you to get a taste of yours. Get your boots on, let the hike up the mountain begin.

ONE-SCOPING OUT YOUR JOURNEY

"This is your journey, your body, your mind, and your spirit. Dig deep, own it and start doing things for you and by you." - Anonymous

"What boots should I wear?" you might ask me. "Will I need a jacket?" If you were hiking in Wisconsin, you would need waterproof boots, a down jacket, and warm mittens. However, not even the most rugged gear will help you with this type of hike. Even a GPS system can't guide you on this trek. No energy drink will sustain you throughout your journey.

Our hike is up the mountain of life. Your destination is a point in time when you've encountered your vision of success, accomplishment, fulfillment, and happiness. Many people attempt this hike, yet only a few make it to the peak.

Let's simplify things. What is the shortest distance between two distinct points? What is the shortest distance from your current position (point A) and the dream life you imagine for yourself (point B)? The answer is a straight line! Unfortunately, the hike in life isn't always that simple. The path to this point B ventures through jungles, through valleys, up steep cliffs, into dark caves, and across thin ice. Point B is at the summit of what looks to be the tallest, most intimidating, and dangerous mountain in existence: life. Note, there isn't a ski lift, fire road, tram, or sled-ride in this world to get us to the top of this mountain.

Unfortunately, knowing the terrain isn't enough for this journey. You must be aware of the different types of life-hikers that have attempted to peak the mountain. That can only be achieved by looking at the mountain from above.

Far off of the path to the top, we would find many *average hikers* clumped in groups. As the average hiker is trekking their way to the top, they make decisions that lead them away from point B. They pull all-nighters, do drugs, overdrink, gossip about others, overeat, get involved in drama, mouth off to authorities, and the list goes on. They don't realize that their character determines 90% of their success. One wrong decision leads to another, and the average hiker has wasted hours, days, months, and eventually years chasing false dreams. Their bad choices pave side trails that are ill-fated and leave them feeling lost and forgetful of the original path they were on. As they confront dead-ends, average hikers eventually realize that they aren't where they want to be. When this happens, their self-confidence drops and they ultimately end up right back where they started, if not behind their starting point. Average hikers are the most common life hikers on the mountain.

Looking further up the mountain, we would find scattered *lonely hikers* struggling to press on. Early on, lonely hikers become consumed by their journey to seek out their dreams. They start incredibly motivated to make it to point B as fast as possible. These hikers forget to bring the proper provisions for their uphill journey. They stay up all night, don't take breaks, sacrifice health for work, and become oblivious to their own body's needs. Their drive can be characterized as self-absorbed and mostly self-serving. Throughout their journey, they ignore the "helping stations" posted along the way for them. Eventually, their "fan bus" is empty, as they have given up spending time with their friends, their family, and all who support them.

Believing that their journey is more important than anything else in the world, these hikers eventually realize that they, too, have become lost, strayed from their original path. Thus, when they confront a blizzard of hard times, they do not have the support they need to stick to the right path. Since selfish gain is one of the only motivations for their journey, lonely hikers lack energy and regularly experience burnout. Having alienated their supporters, lonely hikers have no one to go to for help, which gives them less leverage for conquering their journey. Once too far behind, lonely hikers lose motivation and give up. Not only do they give up, but they blame the world and the people around them for why the journey didn't go their way.

At base camp of the mountain, we would find *jealous hikers*. The jealous hiker is aware of the struggles ahead on the journey to point B, yet is content with making easy decisions and avoiding challenges throughout their life. Settling for mediocrity, the jealous hiker never gains the courage to start their journey. Because they can't see themselves doing something, they can't see anyone else doing it, either. Thus, they talk unfavorably about the hikers making their current journey, calling them arrogant, silly, know-it-alls, and telling themselves that the struggling hikers will never make it anyway. At base camp, they sip hot cocoa with other jealous hikers, gossiping about those who are suffering on their journey up the mountain. In reality, the jealous hiker will never amount to anything. Like the lonely hiker, they perceive the mountain of life to be unfair, cruel, and not worth summiting. The real issue with the jealous hiker is pride. The jealous hiker is so prideful that they will never risk failure by attempting to travel to point B. To encourage themselves, they criticize those who are committed to summiting. Deep down, they are jealous of those with the willpower to struggle to succeed.

The fourth type of hiker is the *content hiker*. Many hikers reach a checkpoint on their journey and are so wrapped up in their success that they decide to slow down or stop hiking. Once they receive recognition, a promotion, raise, job bonus, or anything that they sought when they started their journey, they decide, "This is good enough for me." While content hikers recognize that there is still a potential journey up to the summit, they are so satisfied with where they are and so focused on how far they have come that they begin to coasting. They partake in the "senior slide" of life. Content hikers eventually lose the energy and drive which initially brought them up the mountain and become unhappy. They become despondent because they ignore one crucial fact: success is not a destination, but rather the fuel to continue up the mountain of life.

The last type of hiker is the *persistent hiker*. 100% committed to making it to the summit, the persistent hiker works with and motivates the other hikers around them, continually helps others, and maintains a positive attitude. These tenacious hikers are thankful for their resources and do not waste them. During their journey, the persistent hiker understands that rest is necessary to refuel their minds and bodies for the journey ahead. These hikers choose their friends wisely and understand that persistence is the hiking gear they need to summit. The persistent hiker is early for appointments, proactive about assignments, continually working to improve, and extremely humble in all aspects. While persistent hikers have a clear vision of where point B is and how they will get there, they know that **success is a journey, not a destination.**

Instead of stressing out about their destination, persistent hikers focus on defining and refining their journey - the process. These hikers see mistakes, failures, and struggles as necessary for their journey.

The Power of the Why

Let's pretend that we were able to take a ski lift to the summit of the journey of life. We would find the top of the mountain to be peaceful - lacking wind, rain, and snow. The small group of people at the top would be thankful for the enormous amount of adversity that they confronted on their journey up the mountain.

With no clouds in the sky, we would then notice many courageous hikers at base camp motivated to start their trip. The higher up the mountain we looked, the fewer hikers we would see. It's because only the most dedicated hikers can push through the rough terrain, harsh weather, and the hardships that life throws at them in order to make it to the summit. A few difficulties for hikers on the path of life include a loss of friends, being 'unaccepted,' sacrificing time, feeling lonely, getting burnt out, being rejected, and the like.

What happens when the suffering hits? *Average hikers* give up, *lonely hikers* burn out, *jealous hikers* make excuses, and *content hikers* take their hiking boots off and retreat to their last checkpoint. Around 90% of these hikers abandon their hike because they have no valid reason for enduring their suffering. Many hikers also quit because they have no idea where their point B is.

This insight is invaluable - **you must have an apparent "WHY" for your journey.**

Think of it this way. Your wonderfully structured mind is working to keep you alive. It doesn't want you to suffer! It would prefer that you sit with a bag of Doritos immersed in Netflix rather than hit the gym. It would rather have you sit in the warmth of base camp with the "bros," the "homies," and the "buddies" than get your boots on and start the uphill journey.

For this reason, point B must be clearly defined. A clear definition for point B will help you to find reasons as to why you're enduring your journey. You must have an answer for yourself during times of pain, suffering, and loneliness. In the blizzards of the trip, your mind will ask you, "Why am I up at 1:00 a.m. working on this essay? Why am I at the gym at 5:00 a.m? Why am I spending the weekend on a report rather than hanging out on the beach with my friends?"

When you examine any one of your journeys - whether it be to do well on a test, to become successful one day, to be a better parent - whatever it is - it is vital to ask yourself these questions while scoping your journey.

Where exactly is point B?
Why do I want to get to point B?
How will I possibly suffer on my journey?
Am I willing to stick with the suffering at whatever cost?
What am I willing to sacrifice to reach my summit?

If I've learned anything in my five years of Taekwondo, three years of competitive sparring, five years of gymnastics, and four years at military school, it is the more in-depth and detailed you can answer these questions, the more energy you will have for your journey. Again, you must have the answers to these questions in the back of your mind at all times. Remember, during times of discomfort, your brain will fight against you. Your brain won't want to wake up early, work hard, or do the extra hour of work. Your answers will help you to override the system, reprogram your mind, and become a persistent hiker.

Being a persistent hiker is easier said than done. It's the arduous route that most avoid in their lives. It involves considerable risk, hard work, mental rewiring, yet in due course, an unbeatable reward for those who choose it. I wanted it, and each day I decide to be a *persistent* hiker. But this book isn't about me - it's about you. My goal is to not only inspire your journey but to put you on the path of the *persistent* hiker.

TWO-911, WHAT IS YOUR EMERGENCY?

"It is impossible to live without failing at something unless you live so cautiously that you might as well not have lived at all, in which case you have failed by default." -J.K. Rowling

In fifth grade, I called the police on a school phone as a joke. No, I'm not a "troubled youth." Yet, the off-the-wall things I did throughout elementary and middle school will make it seem like I was a few things: crazy, "spirited" (a mainstream label for out of control), and slightly disturbed. Yes. All three of those. Did I mention weird, socially awkward, and overall a clown? If you read between the lines, I was just a goofy kid looking for acceptance, purpose, and a place to fit in. When you read about how lost I was, you may be able to identify with your own life or the life of another person who feels lost. Hopefully, my mistakes help direct you away from a dead-end, isolated, ambiguous path.

"Skyler, won't you read for us?" my kindergarten teacher politely but firmly commanded. Mrs. Catherine had a soft voice connected to the kindest soul on the face of the earth. Nonetheless, I looked around with an irked expression at the other thirty students sitting on the "reading" carpet.

"I've already finished the book!" I boldly exclaimed. My mom had already taught me to read. I was reading chapter books by the age of four and could not grasp that most kids were just beginning to venture into the world of picture books - how odd! Everyone in the class just gawked at me. I could not accept that for half of the students, this picture book was their first reading experience. I was appalled at the thought that Mrs. Catherine wanted me to read this picture book with a bunch of students who hadn't learned to read yet. Sitting still on a carpet with thirty other students for an hour was already bad enough. Having to read *David Gets in Trouble* made matters even worse. All I wanted to do was go outside and run, run, run. "Come back here, David!" I read at the top of my lungs. "David, be quiet! Don't play with your food. That's enough, David! Go to your room." David wasn't the only one who was sent to timeout before the end of the book.

I dreaded school from kindergarten through seventh grade. My parents had moved us to a sleepy, quaint town known for its outstanding education and family values - a place where the public schools had a stellar reputation coveted by many desiring to raise their families. Little did my parents know, I was often unchallenged, so I channeled my stagnant energy into misbehaving, talking out of turn, disrespecting my teachers, and becoming the class clown all to enhance an ordinary academic school day. I loathed going to school in the mornings, battling it out daily with my mother, who had to plead with me just to get me there each morning. I only looked forward to my accelerated math class in the afternoon. As my attitude toward my teachers worsened, the root of my problems became clear to my parents.

Most public school academics came easy to me. What challenged my awkward self was the social piece - interacting with other students. I resorted to making students laugh in hopes of becoming well-liked. I became the *class clown*.

In first grade, I hurled a milk carton across my lunchroom.

The horrified PTO "lunch mom" found me laughing hysterically under the lunch table several minutes after my carton's launch. In third grade, I read a horror story that I had written in hopes that I would make my classmates laugh. Instead, while reading it to the class, the exuded violence of the story evoked horror in the teacher and students - they became scared of me. In my fourth-grade art class, I played a video of my friend repeatedly saying, "Do it, Max, do it, Max, do it do it do it Max" while the teacher was giving a lecture to my class, only to embarrass myself. In fifth grade, I played a sound on my computer in the middle of English class. In the middle of my teacher's "poetic pause," my laptop spewed, "Get in my belly." In sixth grade, amid a discussion about the constitution, I threw a pencil across the classroom.

Nobody usually laughed. If anyone did, they were just embarrassed for me or laughing *at* me. It wasn't funny. It was embarrassing.

On an early morning in October, I felt deep satisfaction running through my veins as I heard, "911: what is your emergency" coupled with many of my classmates and the girl I had a crush on bursting into hysterical laughter. Sadly, much like the last four girls that had rejected me, she too was not interested in this loser that cracked jokes and acted idiotic for other peoples' acceptance. I still didn't realize that my classmates were not laughing *with* me, but rather *at* me.

From the other side of the classroom, the new substitute teacher turned and glared at me in disbelief. My heart seemed to stop, and my vision narrowed to just the head of my substitute teacher. As I heard the police on speakerphone ask, "Hello? Is anyone there? What is your emergency?" my eyes were locked onto the vague gestures my teacher was making at me.

A wave of nervousness swept over me. For some reason, I had a history of laughing during serious situations: during church services, lectures from my superiors, and worst yet: funerals. At one funeral, I laughed and cried within the same hour!

With the police on the phone, my nervousness surged; I

went from frowning to an outright burst of hysterical laughter. The teacher, awe-stricken, ran across the classroom and quickly snatched the phone out of my hands.

By the time the substitute teacher had taken control of the situation, my bubble of happiness and nervous laughter had deflated. I slowly and shamefully made my way into the hallway, head in my hands. The look in my teacher's eyes mimicked the same look my future Russian gymnastics coach would give me when I was anything less than perfect. His wasn't a look of anger, but a look of profound disappointment. It was the kind of look felt in the depths of one's core. No doubt, Mr. Patrick wanted to let me have it. However, his disapproving feelings for me stopped him from proceeding with what would have been a more than deserving consequence. A blank stare was all I received from him - I'll never forget it. Mr. Patrick decided that ignoring my prank call to the police would be best for both of our school records. I dodged a bullet.

Mr. Patrick understood me. It was an "Ah-ha!" moment. He figured out that for me, being challenged was a detour from an endless road of trouble. Because I felt mentally stretched in fifth grade, I grew. The problematic kid that I was all of a sudden stopped having issues with teachers, assimilated into a peer group, became a more compliant individual at home, and no longer needed his parents to force him to go to school. I was motivated. I had direction.

Who was that old Skyler? I can hardly believe I was capable of that sort of behavior. Sound familiar? Are there instances you can recall that bring forth similar feelings of shame, causing you to blush just by reminiscing your past? We can probably share feelings of thankfulness that, as Bill Keane puts it, "Yesterday is history, tomorrow is a mystery."

It was during my fifth-grade year that my parents acted. They did something that I feel that, if done by all parents in the United States for their children, would reduce crime, poverty, high school drop-out rates, and teenage alcoholism. My parents started to challenge me in all areas of my life. Even more, they didn't let me quit anything. For me, the uncertainty and pressure of a challenge gave me almost the same "thrill" as watching a horror film. The thrill kept me focused on the right things and far from the accustomed clown act.

My two favorite suspense thrillers - *The Sixth Sense* and *The Conjuring* - couldn't come close to the thrill that Taekwondo and gymnastics gave me. It was in these two sports that I learned the value of hard work and discipline over talent. I knew I could never be the best in these sports, so I resorted to being the hardest worker. This mindset spread to other aspects of my life: **"I may not be the most talented person in this class, activity, or sports team, but I will be the hardest worker."** Before I touch on this, we'll look at the earthquake that disrupted my path in middle school.

No Child Left Behind

The No Child Left Behind Act was passed by Congress in 2001 and was enacted by President George W. Bush on January 8th, 2002. It was meant to make the United States internationally competitive in education. It increased the government's role in monitoring the academic progress of schools' students. It put "a special focus on ensuring that states and schools boost the performance of certain groups of students, such as English-language learners, students in special education, underprivileged and minority children, whose achievement, on average, trails their peers."

Schools that did not meet the proficiency level set by their state were threatened with state intervention, losing federal funding, or even closure. While the law, in theory, was helping *all students* to achieve academic greatness, in my opinion, it ended up "dumbing down" classes in many public schools in what many politicians referred to as a "race to the bottom." As teachers were forced to assist students who had no desire to assimilate, the result led to oversized classrooms of 20, 30, and upwards of 40 students, both motivated and unmotivated students grouped into one. Overnight, average performance became the new norm. The bar of mediocrity was now set. That "average" now allows public schools to pass their state proficiency tests.

While my educators tended to students left behind, I would tackle and complete homework from other classes. Many of my teachers were adamant and insisted that I trail with the rest of the class. This constant battle of the wills led to the downfall of my behavior and an unrelenting frustration. There seemed to be an absence of thinking outside the box.

In my sixth and seventh-grade classes, I was assigned weekly homework to complete by the end of the week. When I finished all of the week's homework by Monday evening, my teachers would often become irritated with me because I had "no more work" to do for the remainder of the week.

In my sixth-grade science class, the teacher would have the class draw in their science notebooks each month; it was to parallel what was covered in the assigned unit and to be turned in at the end of the month. I always had the assignment done after one weekend. I didn't have time in the evenings to do homework. Once school ended at 3:30 p.m., my life of gymnastics began: practice from 4:00 p.m. to 9:30 p.m. daily. The forty-minute drive there and back, which I typically used to do outstanding assignments, left me starting my projects and exam studying every night around 10:30 p.m. My fuel was the drive-thru fast food I stuffed my face with en route home. My team of educators did not accept such an explanation, eventually putting me on detention for "noncompliance to classroom rules" and "disrespect to authority."

Speak Up

In my seventh grade "Speak Up" class, I was assigned to do a presentation of my choosing. Because the use of headphones was prohibited in class, I did my presentation on "Music and the Brain." In the presentation, I explained how music improves cognitive function and is beneficial to students while studying. The assignment was completed 27 days before the due date. When the teacher noticed I was now attempting to tackle other homework during *his* classroom time, he became incensed.

"Skyler Chauff!" he hollered across the auditorium, "Bring your computer and come sit by me." I complied begrudgingly. An attribute that describes me to the T was that I was hugely flippant. I often responded with a curt short-answer response to anyone I felt wronged me in any way; I reciprocated with sarcastic disdain. I was hardly a "respectful student."

The teacher was thin, tall, and had librarian-looking glasses. He approached me, cocked his head, and glared at me. I knew this look all too well. "You know you are *not* allowed to do anything in this class except for my work. We've gone over this before!" he bitterly exclaimed with a condescending tone. Every eye in the class was on me.

"Yes, but I'm finished with my presentation," I uttered. Here's where my arrogance reared its ugly head. I opened my computer, quickly switched tabs, and showed him the presentation. A sense of satisfaction took over - it felt good, really good. I could tell by his expression that he was impressed. I looked up at him, and after confirming my suspicions, I proceeded to speak unapologetically, "I don't have any more work to do for your class."

"Well, whose fault is that?" the teacher stammered.

In disbelief, I put my head in my hands. I could not comprehend that I was getting scolded for using my own classroom time for what I wanted to do even though I completed the project that was due *next month*. I became increasingly frustrated. I felt my pulse intensifying as I glared at the teacher's face with contempt.

With haughty eyes and with a disrespectful tone, I spewed. "I'm sick of these crazy rules. Why on earth are you mad at me for having my work done?!"

"You, my friend, have earned detention!!!" he yelled as he handed me the all-too-familiar pink slip to get signed by my mother - the slip of shame.

That was my third detention earned in seventh grade, the second from this teacher. Quite honestly, I almost didn't show up to that detention. At the time, I didn't know how I would even look at that teacher again.

As I became more and more disillusioned by *the system* and labeled by my educators, I began acting out in class. I doubled down on my class-clown act. Silly and trivial activities started to distract me. My behavioral grades plummeted, tainting my flawless academic record. Although I was anal about getting all my assignments turned in and done with pride, my overall grades somehow did not reflect the quality of work. It puzzled me. Slowly, my love for learning started to erode. I received detentions for disrupting class, taking other students off-task, and disrespecting teachers. With 28 - 35 students in each of my classes, I didn't know my teachers well. The teachers I knew best were those I spoke with during detention.

One such teacher was Mrs. Smith - the best teacher I ever had. During my last year at public school - seventh grade - she put me in my place. No doubt, I gave her a run for her money and fought tooth and nail for *my* will to be done. When she lowered the behavioral scores of my friends and me, the five of us led a charge to the principal's office - Mrs. Smith was going to pay. I planned to persuade the principal to have Mrs. Smith fired. "She can't just lower our grades because of poor behavior!" we protested, "This is warranted nowhere in school policy!" Looking back, my behavior warranted an F or at the very best, a D. Fortunately for me, as the merciful and wise teacher that she was, Mrs. Smith took me under her wing and nurtured my love to learn; she turned me into an avid writer and reader. During one of my detentions, she decided to challenge me with extra meaningful work. The results were monumental. During the last trimester of Mrs. Smith's class, I brought my C- up to a solid A. Along with this, my grades in other courses improved.

In spite of the several detentions and altercations I encountered with this teacher, I learned something that military school would further harness as a vital attribute: respect for authority.

THREE-A PARENT'S PERSPECTIVE: HE SAID, SHE SAID

"**H**e said *what???!!!*" My mother responded as she sat at my third-grade conference. Silence. Questions. Then came the tears. The tears, according to my mother, were quite typical after one of my parent-teacher meetings. Oh, how my mother dreaded those discussions She would always gear up for them and make sure there were no surprises. Before every conference, it was the same question. "Now, Skyler, is there anything I need to know before meeting with your teacher?" she'd always ask.

Mom always looked the part - dressed in slacks that were pressed just so with a nice jacket to compliment her figure. I never understood why she wore shoes with heels; my mother is a tall woman who exudes confidence. Was it for intimidation purposes? Was it to compliment the outfit? Whatever the reason, Mom's demeanor always demanded respect and authority. Perhaps the heels gave her a boost of confidence during those conferences. I may never really know. Her hair was quickly but neatly tossed back into a messy bun. She looked more like a business professional rather than the typical stay-at-home Mom.

My mother ran a business for years, but she still managed to be present at all of my gymnastics practices, Taekwondo tournaments, and piano lessons. I remember her high energy as she'd run from activity to activity with me. I was her only child at the time, so I suppose she wanted to be as involved as possible in my endeavors. Whether volunteering or coaching or even participating herself, she somehow got involved. I remember when I talked her into doing Taekwondo with me. "Come on Mom! You can do it, and we can do it together! Please?!?!? PLEASE?!!?" I pleaded. It didn't take much; she was always up for a challenge. Several years later and several broken bones healed, both my mother and I became first and second-degree black belts in the Korean discipline of Taekwondo.

Before conferences, I always reassured Mom that there was nothing I was aware of and crossed my fingers, hoping to God that I was right. She approached the door with hesitation and skepticism in her walk. Making her way to the car, she looked me straight in the eyes. I knew that look all too well. It was a look of, "please don't disappoint me - not this time." She was on her way to meet with my teachers.

"Are you sure that's what you heard? Is it possible you may have misunderstood?" The words came out clumsily, riddled with desperation.

"Mrs. Chauff, I'm positive. I'm so sorry to have to share this with you, but I just felt you had to know. As Skyler's teacher, it's important that I make you aware of the things I'm seeing so that collaboratively we can help him." It was a nice way of saying, "Your kid is a handful, and it's my job to let you know.

I could hear the keys in the door jingling as my mother fumbled to make her way into the house. The door swung open, and I could hear her belt out in a loud voice, "Bert! Skyler! We need to talk!" Well, she was past the sobbing stage, and now clearly she was at the anger stage of grief.

"I refuse to go to another conference for him! This is humiliating!" Yep, she was stuck in the anger stage of grief, alright. She was inconsolable.

My mother, born of Greek descent, comes from a "big, fat, Greek family." Passion is her middle name. When she speaks, it's usually with conviction and rarely meek. I don't know why I would expect this situation to be any different. She was living out her heritage; she was hot-tempered. Dad, on the other hand, was always the calm one in MOST situations (I say "most" because I had a way of pushing his buttons from time to time and catching him out of character).

My father, in his typically calm demeanor, tried desperately to extinguish what had erupted before my mother's arrival. "Everybody calm down, what happened? Let me guess, the conference didn't go so well?" My father knew something awful had happened, and before he could even get the words out, he was abruptly interrupted. I didn't dare look over at my mother. There was no need to - I could feel the heat in the room and the tension-filled air. Mom was about to blow!

Mom glared at dad. "*Your* son has no respect for anyone! We have a real problem here that isn't going away. We need to do something radical and now..." I tried to think hard as to what could have happened. What did I do or say? I honestly couldn't remember, but I had a feeling the refresher was coming.

My father felt that it would be a good idea if I went to my room. I concurred. I nervously and quietly made my way up the stairs. I clung to the door with my ear pressed against it making sure I could hear every word my parents were saying. My mother demanded to be heard.

My father was raised on a farm in a small rural community down south. He, too, came from a large family - a cajun one full of mystery and culture. He's witty, smart, unassuming, and, for the most part, laid back. According to my mother, too laid back, and their arguments usually stemmed from their opposite beliefs on child-rearing. Mom grew up in a strict household where her father ran a very tight ship. Dad, on the other hand, lost his father at the age of 12 to a heart attack and was raised by his sisters; his mother was too sick to care for him. His mother knew there was something about him that was special, so she sent him away to school so he could find himself and succeed. This he did. However, Dad isn't big on discipline - that was usually left to my mother.

Dad was always the calm before the storm. He has a way with words and somehow manages to get his point across and eloquently so. People of all backgrounds and walks of life are somehow mesmerized with him. I guess you just have to know him to get the full grasp of what I'm attempting to describe. Without sounding cliche, my dad has taught me many things and continues to do so. He's my rock and my inspiration in so many ways. Though not big into sports, my dad has emulated hard work and success throughout my childhood years. My work ethic today is a product of his example each day. I suppose I inherited some good and some not-so-good genes from both parents. So wildly different, they each have characteristics worthy of imitation.

My attitudes and behaviors were an obvious problem early on in life, it was then, however, when I began to see the magnitude of this flawed character. From there, it only escalated as the years went by. My mother could be heard across the street as her temper got the best of her.

"Mrs. Chauff, Skyler is a knowledgeable young man with a bright future ahead of him. However, several days ago when I assigned groups for this project, I paired him up with two other peers I felt would be suitable and well-matched for him. As I looked around to make sure all the kids were partnered up and working well together, I saw that Skyler went off on his own - he was working on the group project by himself. I decided to give him some time to approach his peers, but rather than working with the two students assigned to him, I instead found Skyler unphased and working independently even after all the other kids were working in groups. I finally approached him and asked him why he wasn't working with his partners. Skyler looked at me, paused for a while, sighed, and finally said, 'Really Mrs. Ross, you put me with dumb and dumber?' Mrs. Chauff, I don't know what to make of that, but I'm concerned enough to bring it to your attention."

As early on as this was, it was just the beginning. For as I excelled, my respect for authority and those around me began to diminish. My mother was quite perceptive and knew early on that I had to be taught respect and humility. Though I genuinely believe the answer in her mind was not a military school, the idea when it presented itself was one she was very open to by the time I started seventh grade.

Brochures of various military academies started popping up around the house. I picked one up in particular and started frantically skimming through the pamphlet. "What is this?" I facetiously asked.

"This is where you will go if you don't clean up your act," Mom calmly and firmly stated.

"Dad will never let it happen," I confidently shot back.

"We'll see about that," Mom mumbled under her breath as she turned and walked away. She knew that something had to change, and if that something was military school, then so be it.

The Perfect School

Despite my successes in accomplishing additional book reports and writing authentic poems for Mrs. Smith, I still had a great deal to learn. My behavior at school was a reflection of my behavior at home. My parents hinted at the possibility of me attending a boarding school. *Nonsense*, I thought. My parents found St. John's Northwestern Military Academy. Recommended by a family therapist and counselor, we decided to take a visit at the end of my seventh grade school year.

Through my seventh-grade eyes, St. John's looked like a 13th century, "prison-castle." I recall when I first walked into the doors of the "Command Post," I saw what looked like two military soldiers. The Command Post is the reception area of the military academy. This was no ordinary reception desk, however. Around this desk were statues, paintings, and the crest - to be given the utmost respect and not to be stepped on. It turned out that the students at the "Command Post" were actually in eighth grade. My parents and I stared at them. They kept their eyes locked and fixated in front of them, hands in a fist at their sides, with bodies, erect in a statuesque-like state. Both students were wearing the exact same uniform: a white dress shirt with a nametag, a yellow star, and a black patch "rank" on their shoulders. *Weird*, I thought. When I walked in front of the students, one of them proudly said, "good afternoon, sir." His greeting sent chills down my spine and reminded me of an episode of *Goosebumps* I had watched before - *the Perfect School*.

In the show, Brian O'Connor is a misfit teen characterized by his contentious relationship with his parents. His parents, acting in his *best interests*, send him to "The Perfect Boarding School." When he arrives at the reformatory institution, he steps off the bus and meets the uniform-dressed "graduates" of the Academy. The graduates acted so politely and courteous that they seemed almost robotic.

When Brian breaks the rules at the school, the academy staff make him go to the "Pattern Room." There, he is weighed and measured. He later discovers that the school replaces the students with identical robots while locking the authentic students in jail cells in the basement. The robots that return home give parents exactly what they want - submissive, compliant, "perfect" sons. Luckily, Brian escapes and manages to find his way home to his parents, thwarting his robot's plans to take over his spot in the family.

I frowned at the cadets manning the Command Post. Why do they stand like that? Why are they so polite? I could feel a headache coming on. My thoughts continued to race with all sorts of questions cluttering my brain. *Do they do everyday activities that other "normal kids" find enjoyable like play video games or watching TV?* I wondered. I couldn't possibly understand what motivated their behavior. It was mystifying.

I was *not* about to end up like them. I was *not* going to turn into a robot. I would *not* be locked away in a cell and replaced.

I didn't know the first thing about military school. My misconceptions came from watching *The Perfect School*, *Full Metal Jacket*, and *Top Gun*. I made up my mind - I most certainly and unequivocally would *not* end up in the "perfect school."

Typing, Taekwondo, and Gymnastics

It's incredible what a typing class, the discipline of Taekwondo, and competitive gymnastics can do for someone's character. Especially for me - I was that stubborn mule, the dog that wouldn't learn new tricks, and that horse that refused to drink the water.

In school, I habitually ignored and disrespected the lunch moms that instructed me not to throw snowballs, among other things, during recess. I rebelled against authority because I wanted to run the show. Although I could read chapter books in kindergarten, I didn't have the discipline to read about a friendship between a pig named Wilbur and a spider named Charlotte, let alone write a summary about it too! I didn't have the self-control to stop eating after just three or four Oreos; I wanted the entire box.

During the summer before sixth grade, I pleaded and begged my mom to allow me to take the summer class that the rest of my friends' parents were enrolling their kids in: fantasy baseball. My pleading fell on deaf ears. Instead, she enrolled me in a typing class for the entire summer. For the three days before the course, I moped around in an effort to change Mom's mind as she repeatedly relayed time and time again, "one day, you will thank me, son." I was sure this was to be the start of a horrible summer.

On the first day of summer school, I begrudgingly walked

into class and glared at the teacher - Mrs. Keys. *How perfect*, I facetiously thought, *her name was Mrs. Keys*. When she greeted me, I gave her a piercing look. Every day for three hours, I sat in a classroom and learned "the art of typing." As I sat in front of a keyboard doing typing exercises, I could see my friends right outside the window enjoying their "fantasy baseball" class. I didn't care if typing class would help me. Quite honestly, I didn't see the meaning behind finger exercises, typing games, and the class favorite - presentations. I was jealous of my friends, annoyed with the teacher, and angry at my mom.

Placing me in typing class, Taekwondo, and gymnastics was the start of the "taming of the shrew." The beginning of the end - an effort on my parent's part to bridle their wild horse. Just like that, the next chapter of my life was about to bestow me.

Stubborn Fool

I was a stubborn fool. Now I'm just stubborn about different things. When you're stubborn about the right stuff, the things that lead you up the path to the peak, then there is hope! Let's look at Jack. Jack was stubborn about becoming popular in high school. So stubborn that he foolishly took steroids, drank alcohol, smoked weed, and skipped school just to fit in. Where did he end up? Jack was extremely popular in high school. He graduated at the bottom of his class, attended community college, and eventually dropped out. He worked at a fast-food restaurant for several years, was fired for being high on the job, and never sought employment again. To this day, Jack solicits for money on the streets of Chicago. He spends his earnings on drugs and alcohol.

Stubborn Fool #1

Another stubborn man was told he was 'too stupid to learn anything' by his teachers in school. He went on to become

America's "greatest inventor," receiving 1,093 patents. Most notably the phonograph, the light bulb, and the motion picture. Thomas Edison also started more than 14 companies and is known as one of the most productive men in American history. One of his employees eloquently described how he stubbornly spent 60 consecutive hours solving a problem he was having with a printing machine.

In this book, I'll challenge you. I'll challenge you to achieve the vision you have for yourself. Thomas Edison was on day three, hour fifty-five without sleep, and he still couldn't manage to solve a problem. How discouraged do you think he felt?

However, Edison viewed failure differently than most of us do. "I have not failed. I've just found 10,000 ways that won't work," he said. How discouraged were you the last time you came to a roadblock? Did you quit? Maybe push off that challenge for a few days, weeks, months, or years?

Stubborn Fool #2

Another stubborn man didn't start speaking until he was four years old and reading until he was seven. His professors rarely took him seriously. He failed out of several math courses, almost dropped out of school, was regarded by his dad as a complete failure, and had trouble finding employment after college. Later in his life, his academic peers labeled him crazy. He went on to divorce his wife and ultimately lost his family. Albert Einstein went on to prove his teachers and the scientific community wrong. In 1921, Einstein received the Nobel Prize in Physics. He is best known for his Theory of Relativity.

Most know Edison as a successful inventor and Einstein as a successful physicist. I'll bet most are unaware of their arduous journeys to success, their pitfalls along the way that rarely took center stage. Look, you will inevitabl**y fail** at some point. You **will mess up.** You **will be embarrassed** along the way. When all of this transpires, you **will want to quit.** This is part of your journey to success! You have to embrace it and **move forward!!** Failure is the prelude **to success.** You become that "stubborn fool." I dare you.

Discipline?

Before middle school, I couldn't appreciate the concept of discipline: forgoing instant gratification to better myself - what? Failure until success? Before military school, if you walked up to me and mentioned that I needed discipline, I would direct you to the nearest mental health hospital Back to my point. The "gains" from the dreaded typing class presented its return at the end of middle school and high school. Now, being able to type a simple 100 words per minute, I can breeze through high school essays and papers. One "lost" summer was equivalent to hours, days, weeks, and probably months gained from finishing work ahead of schedule. Without that typing class, chances are you wouldn't be reading this book right now.

My mother also enrolled me in Taekwondo and sparring classes. Round-house kicks, side-kicks, grueling leg workouts, dreaded calisthenics, burpees, and long routines started filling up my nights. Then (against my will), I had to learn and engage in sparring. Imagine an undisciplined, negative, cocky, and disrespectful middle schooler competing in his first state-wide sparring competition. Oh, and let me add, the thought of losing never crossed my mind! I got my butt, as well as my self-esteem, kicked in the first round. Three seconds into the round, and after laughing at my opponent, a foot slammed into my head. It brought me and my ego to the ground.

I was also doing gymnastics, the sport that replaced Taekwondo at age ten. Gymnastics became my new obsession.

I just loved the aspect of conditioning every muscle in my body to accomplish a common goal: seamless control and acrobatic flow. Unfortunately, as I progressed in my ability as a gymnast, I regularly became injured. My wrists, back, shoulders, arms, and hands began deteriorating. My doctors soon realized that gymnastics was stunting my growth.

Here's where things get interesting. It wasn't learning a routine on the rings or being able to do a double backflip on the floor that scared me, but rather the instruction from my gymnastics coaches. Often, when I did things wrong, I was called "stupid boy."

I'll be frank. Ten-year-old, cocky, fresh out of the sparring match Skyler was not ready to be called stupid. Though I portrayed a tough-as-nails exterior, deep down, I was thin-skinned and desperate for approval.

When corrected, I would sneak out to the bathroom, cry, and feel sorry for myself. You can bet I cut that out real quick after I fared poorly in my first year of competitions. The following year, however, I started taking constructive criticism to heart. I used it to my benefit by turning negative thoughts into positive affirmations and thus replacing the fruitless negative cycle in my brain. I knew I was not the best gymnast on my team, but I was determined to be the most driven and hardest working because, at the very least, I could control that. So that's what I did, and that's who I became. That drive and tenacity earned me the respect of my coaches.

Okay, now that you've made it this far, **I have to let you in on a secret**. I'm pretty crazy. By crazy, I mean compulsively obsessed. I earned the nickname "crazy boy" at my gym. My Russian coaches continually had to remind me to "be chill" when I was unable to master a skill on my timeline.

During one practice on the pommel horse, I was unable to complete a full rotation on the apparatus. I mentally chastised myself, relentlessly pushing until I was able to complete a full rotation. Only when I was on the brink of complete exhaustion did I understand the theory my coaches had been trying to enlighten me with: quality over quantity.

During another practice, I couldn't master the "press." This skill entails starting in a straddle position in an attempt to lift one's legs to a handstand position. By using the strength of one's core, you then proceed to use your hands to prop up your body and keep it from falling over. Because of my clumsy, taller stature, doing this was close to impossible. For thirty minutes, I tried pushing myself up without resting. Only when I was on the verge of tears and muscle failure did my coach enter the scene. He slipped in "stupid boy" at the end of what he told me, but I knew he meant well. I needed to quit feeling sorry for myself and work smarter, not harder. I didn't realize how to do this until later on in high school when burnout would consume other facets of my life.

I was not the best gymnast on the team like I was at my old gym. I had gone from being a big fish in a small pond to a small fish in a big pond. As a small fish, I still thought I was a big shot. I was nothing now.

It was almost like I just moved from high school to college athletics - a vast difference. Unfortunately, due to a chain of injuries coupled with my genetics, I took longer to master skills and progress.

At around 5'7, I was the tallest gymnast in my entire gym - just a seventh-grader. One of my Russian coaches, who had an enormous amount of respect for me, pulled my mom aside one day. Years later, my mom revealed what he had told her. "I can see that this is Skyler's passion. I'm amazed that he is one of the hardest working gymnasts I have ever seen in my thirty years of instructing. Unfortunately, you must know he is too tall to continue for much longer." He expressed this to her the summer before seventh grade. Mom decided to keep this to herself. One year later, I was standing tall in military formation.

One morning, I walked into my family room. "What's up?" I asked. You could hear the trepidation in my voice. That, along with my nervous laughter, was driven by my anxiety. A decision was about to be revealed. My parents, talking *at* me as if they had been discussing my fate for the last few hours, looked pleased to see me nervous. Although I didn't realize it at the time, this conversation was the catalyst for the next five years of my life. I wish I could relay the details of that conversation. Unfortunately, I was too busy zoning in and out.

As my parents went through all of the mundane benefits of military school - how it would help my future, get me into an exceptional college, blah blah blah. Their voices became like white noise. The only sound I could hear was my thought process going round and round like a Ferris wheel. I thought of all I would be leaving behind: my friends, family, my first girlfriend, my comfortable bed and familiar room, the endless supply of grandma's pancakes on Saturdays, and worst of all, my weekends. My head was spinning.

I envisioned a cadet drill sergeant screaming at the top of his lungs to scrub the dust off of his floor with a toothbrush at 4:00 a.m. However, I also knew I was at a crossroads. I rationalized, I'm too tall for gymnastics anyways. I then looked mom and dad in the eyes and responded, "I'll try it."

Truthfully, the almost two-hour drive over to the campus was unnerving. It was like waiting in line for an amusement park ride that your friend coerced you to go on.

The night before registration day, or what I jokingly refer to as "D-Day," my parents and I arrived at a hotel near the academy. I lugged in what little belongings I packed, and sauntered into the doors of the hotel. I was as insecure and scared, camouflaged by an arrogance. My mom then proceeded to do what she does best - embarrass me. She exclaimed, "Hiiiii," in her charming demeanor, ran over, and started small talk conversation with an unfamiliar father and son team. Almost immediately, she joyfully discovered that this young man was also attending St. John's. Across the bustling hotel reception lobby, my mother emphatically shouted: "Skyler, come over here and say hello!" There was no getting out of it, so I methodically and begrudgingly made my way over, managed to rehearse some small talk in my head, and proceeded with a feeble attempt to introduce myself to this fellow peer. "Hey, I'm Skyler... what's your name?"

There, I stood in front of my first roomate. My first friend at military school. My best friend at military school. He had done competitive gymnastics and was an avid martial artist.

"Hey man, I'm Tommy," he responded.

Tommy would stick by my side as an ally for the next two and a half years. He would become my "battle-buddy." Even against the heavy gunfire of situations equatable to the Battle of the Bulge (New Cadet Training), he would put me on his shoulders and hoist me up. He was the kind of friend who would always take the blame for me, loyal to a fault, despite the consequences.

The verbal, physical, mental, and emotional stresses of new cadet D-Day were near. However, I see now that D-Day was a necessary part of my path, my journey, and my mountain.

FOUR-D-DAY

"Here's a news flash: No soldier gives his life. That's not the way it works. Most soldiers who make a conscious decision to place themselves in harm's way do it to protect their buddies. They do it because of the bonds of friendship - and it goes so much deeper than friendship." - Eric Massa

Massa's words give us the overture of military school. Military school is a challenge. It is demanding. It summons students academically, physically, mentally, and emotionally. Doesn't that sound fun? Probably not the kind of fun most people have in mind.

Keep reading.

How do you think that I, a lost eighth-grader and cocky gymnast, could get through it? Why do so many students in this environment follow suit and decide to stick with this challenge?

There's a reason why those who attend military school have faith in the program and end up loving it. They discover that it's an alternative kind of fun. It's the kind of fun that marathon runners train for night and day. It's the bottom line that CEOs chase after. It's the ultimate goal that many world leaders seek. It's an everlasting type of gratification, one more deeply satisfying than any alcoholic beverage, antidepressant drug, or Krispy Kreme donut. Be careful. This type of amusement dangerously injects purpose, fulfillment, and motivation through the veins of those who find it.

This gratification precedes and accompanies hard work. It's the feeling you get when you know you are working on or working towards something meaningful. It's a feeling that grasps the hiker throughout his journey to hard-earned success. Don't believe me? Ask the marathon runner who won first place or the CEO who was named in Forbes top 10 movers and shakers of corporate America. What about the most powerful leader of the free world turning around a stagnant economy into a booming one - ask them to express how *that* accomplishment feels.

Most of us run from this type of "fun." But, like a drug, it can be contagious through the right kind of peer pressure. Specifically, persistent hiker pressure. This "fun" at military school likely wouldn't be possible without the cohesiveness among the cadets!

In military school, each student becomes part of a brotherhood. A brotherhood that extends to every, single, student. A brotherhood that includes those with glasses, those who stutter, those from foreign countries, and yes, those who are considered "nerds." The chain of brotherhood remains linked after five, ten, twenty, and even thirty years after the machine that made the chain is gone. Don't believe me? Come to a St. John's graduation ceremony and watch as 70-year-old men continue to bond over their best military school moments.

I'll tell you a quick story that displays the unconditional love of the brotherhood. There was a student I sat near in Spanish class. I'll call him "Johnny." Almost daily, Johnny disrupted class, annoyed and distracted his peers, came to class unprepared, and aggravated the teacher. I can still picture him - his thin, petite body - crawling under the desks during the middle of a lesson. He would grab limbs as he weaved his way around like a slippery snake. I can still hear him giggling under his breath. What on earth? He claimed to have forgotten his meds that day. Without a doubt - he annoyed *everybody* to no end. He definitely tested my patience.

One day, Johnny was reprimanded for a less-than-fair situation. From what I can remember, it was something as minuscule as showing up to class late. We were a small class of students representing three different countries. Despite the fact that Johnny annoyed us to no end, we decided that it was only right to stick up for him, even if it meant challenging the teacher. We concurred he was still one of us... he was a brother.

Wrong School?

My head was spinning with doubt: I must've been at the wrong school. Maybe my parents had taken the wrong turn. "What did I even sign up for?"

The scattered, antiquated cannons and the immediate sight of new students marching through the school's quad left me walking through a warzone in my imagination. I thought about the 130-year history of the campus and the structure that so proudly stands on its well maintained and almost perfectly manicured grounds.

Large, black and grey gravestones disperse the quad, which looked up to the towering, 200-foot flag pole. Each stone represents a previous graduating class. In the middle of the quad, the 'guard path' road brought me to the base of the flagpole. The view of the campus beyond the quad was almost overwhelming. Directly in view from the flagpole was the parade field, the football field, and a golf course.

Amidst the drill commands echoing throughout campus, my brain was a sponge, absorbing everything all around me in this foreign war zone. Only, this "war zone" was made up of motivated seventh - twelfth graders functioning under a rank structure, placed in leadership positions, and housed in century-old dorms known as "the barracks." Out of the corner of my eye, I noticed several students standing erect like unbending pencils in a perfectly formed line. They each wore a pressed white shirt, checkered black trousers, long black socks, and black, leather, low quarter shoes. One onlooker made gestures to try to make them flinch. Nobody did except a Chinese student with the name "Moon" written on his nametag. He made a half-smile which was immediately scolded by what was called, "Cadet Command." Right behind Moon stood a sign which appropriately exclaimed: "Run for your life." Yes, that's exactly what crossed my mind.

Surely this is a mistake. How was learning to stand erect and move upon command part of the "Academic promise, team-building activities, and regular paintball tournaments" that the school's website mentioned? Everyone smiled and seemed to be having "fun" on the promotional video. I was observing the antithesis of excitement... these individuals seemed stoic. I suddenly felt my mouth go dry as I stroked my furrowed brow. "Dad," I whispered, "I think we made a mistake." He snickered under his breath. An older, self-assured man in a camo uniform looked in my direction and smiled. When our eyes met, I made an awkward gesture of acknowledgement but soon regretfully put my hand back in my pocket. I acted as if I was reaching for something. My face started to blush as I shut my eyes, turned around, and acted like I was telling my dad something. Camo-man waltzed away.

There I was again, awkward looking, out of sorts, and scared out of my mind. I didn't dare let on, so I hid behind the guise of arrogance. After several conversations, hugs, and tearful goodbyes, all the middle schoolers were rounded up and given instructions from the "Cadet Command."

1. You will get into three spaced out lines called a formation. (*Oh, now we were officially getting lined up for the slaughterhouse*).

2. You will stand at the position of attention with your arms at your side, your hands in a fist, and with your eyes locked forward. (*Cattle are too stubborn to stand still*).

3. You will not be able to itch, talk, or move your eyes.

Hold on. What?!! I looked for my dad's vehicle. Gone. As I reached for my phone to call my parents, I looked at Tommy. He too looked shocked absorbing the orders barked at us. "I'm from Texas. I don't take instructions from this goofy 'Cadet Command.' Get me an adult." I felt a sigh of relief knowing I wasn't alone - someone else felt just as uneasy.

I looked to my left. A cadet leader stood close to my face. "Get to attention, new cadet." He continued. "Redboard!" I could *never* get used to that name. New Cadet? Redboard? *Okay*, I thought, *this is lunacy*. They need to treat me like a human being. I could put up with "stupid boy." But this? No way, no how.

A student with a black, cowboy-like hat told me in a southern accent to get into the "Front-leaning rest." I glared back at him with a confused yet arrogant smile.

"What are you talking about?" I asked.

"Push the earth!"

I wasn't too good at making friends and often shied away from large social situations. I encountered many awkward moments. In my insecurity, I often stuttered, relayed the opposite of what I wanted to express, or sometimes laughed at the wrong times. I inherited a nervous laugh that reared its head at the worst possible moments. I remember how a rebuke from my Russian gymnastics coach turned into a long personalized lecture - I just couldn't control that nervous laugh and it got me into some trouble. How about this as a strategy - maybe if I made the people around me laugh, they would want to be my friends. It didn't work at public school. It probably wasn't going to work at military school. It only brought me grief.

I laughed hesitantly, "But I can't do that, it's floating through space."

I looked over at Tommy, expecting him to laugh. No response. Maybe it was just a bad joke. I looked back at "Cadet Command" and put on the cool smile that was my casual wear throughout middle school. I could feel the tension of the situation escalating. Several other cadets with "cowboy" hats and multiple chevrons on their ranks began to approach my thin, pale figure, which looked out of place under the wave of the overwatching American flag.

It all came to me at once. Three different hands pointed at me with straightforward loud instructions. "Get on the ground, son! Do what he told you! Who do you think you are?!"

"I am Skyler Angelo Chauff!!!!"

A small amount of spit sprayed into my left eye as he continued. "What have you earned? Nothing! You are a redboard! You don't deserve anything!"

I got on the ground. "One!!!!" I yelled, "Two!!!!... Ten!!!!"

Ten was just the beginning.

I got back up. I stood up straight - just like a pencil.

An Intro to the Lingo

In the military, there exists a legion of **non-commissioned officers** (NCOs) and **officers**. While the officers typically plan, draft, and prepare for events, the NCO's execute, and are known as the "backbone" of the Army, to say the least. Both groups work together in order to execute their objectives. In a typical unit, such as a battalion, the highest-ranking officer and NCO, the First Captain and Command Sergeant Major (CSM), collaborate with each other while taking charge of their particular 'legion.' At St. John's, the Battalion CSM is often chosen for being the most daunting cadet on campus. Unfortunately for me, I made my first impression with the wrong person.

Command Sergeant Major Jim's first assignment after receiving his position was to identify those cadets who needed haircuts. I was on that list. Although I had told my hairstylist back home that I needed a "military-style haircut," I failed to pass the inspection. At once I was ordered to the barber's room, where I was assembled into a separate formation. I was one of many lucky recipients of the "Number 1 Special," a haircut also known as the "buzz cut." Tommy and I snickered as we meandered toward the barber's line, hopefully away from Cadet Command.

As we waited, I saw new cadets, like myself, walking out of the barber's domain in disbelief. Christened with their new military-style cuts, many of them possessed a displaced look on their faces while feeling for stubs in the place of where their summer hairdos once flowed.

In front of me, Kevin Moon, a friend and true mentor who to this day I still keep in touch with, shared what we called a "nervous laughter" in anticipation of our military-grade haircuts. Here's the worst thing about this nervous laugh - it was contagious! It didn't take much for someone else's laugh to trigger my nervous laugh... Kevin was the instigator today.

Kevin Moon had his eyes set on the stars. A voracious reader, he was always focusing on self-improvement and accomplishing his goals. He was and still is one of my primary sources of inspiration. With his extravagant and cultured hairstyle, Kevin was almost in tears about losing his hair. Behind me, Tommy, my ally, stood gawking at the cadets who emerged looking like what he termed as "burn victims."

There was only one member of "Cadet Command" nearby. Kevin, Tommy, and I took that to our advantage and laughed at those who emerged from the barber's office. Kevin and I, skittish to lose what we had spent time growing over the summer, felt a nervous laugh sweep over us. Cadet Command somehow made their way over to us in order to keep us in line with the position of attention - erect pencil position. Kevin and I mocked the leaders who were watching over our section of the barber line. We saluted with the wrong hand, made frowning faces, and laughed whenever anyone was ordered to do push-ups.

That's when CSM approached me again. At the time, he was a senior in high school. He was the Raider-Team Commander - the military school equivalent of being the captain of the football team. Let me tell you a little something about this guy. He's someone worthy of respect. Recently, he completed a 140-mile hike from Green Bay to Milwaukee, Wisconsin while carrying rucksacks in order to raise awareness for veteran suicide. Yet, I took it upon myself to disrespect him.

At the time, however, he seemed like an ordinary kid who thought he was "tough." What did I know? I had no idea of what respect and authority looked like.

"Cadet Chauff!" CSM Jim yelled, "I don't like your attitude! Why are you talking? You think this is some sort of joke?"

Well yes, as a matter of fact, I did think this was a joke. I thought the entire idea of standing still in a line, silent, unable to look around, smirk, or even move was a joke. I was not about to vocalize this in front of everyone. As had happened with me in the past when my Russian coach would stand my teammates and me against a wall and call us "stupid boys," a smirk emerged from my face. My mother once told me that she avoided bringing me to funerals and wakes as much as possible. She never knew when my nervous laugh would rear its ugly head.

My smirk became more pronounced as I looked at the stern face of the cadet who had just claimed himself to be "an authority - my authority." Unfortunately, as I had learned, the laughter of others (Kevin), as well as the further aggravation of the "authority," would only exacerbate my distasteful idiosyncrasy. Finally, Kevin's hysterical outburst resonated with me and I proceeded to burst into laughter, right in front of several NCOs, camo-dressed adults, and of course, CSM Jim.

"Nope. Not a joke." I gasped. This was a big mistake. Laughing at the CSM and then failing to address him by his title when I responded was like calling a policeman "bro" when pulled over. Not good.

The CSM next glared at me with a menacing face, which, in and of itself, provoked me to stutter. "W-W-W-Why can't I talk when I feel like it? Really? This is stupid. Who on earth do you think you are?"

Seconds later, the CSM and his other cadet NCOs gathered

around me again and ordered me to do pushups. These yowling NCOs, who I now have appreciation for, would keep me on a track of constant discipline for the next year.

Cadet CSM barked at me. "I am the Command Sergeant Major. I remember when I was in your shoes, feeling all tough. Someday you'll realize, little man. Now get down and do some pushups!" Only after I replied with an exuberant yet sarcastic, "Sure thing, Sergeant Command Major," with a purposeful cough, did I get down to do pushups, as ordered. It was commonplace for me to get the last word in.

A seasoned gymnast and martial artist, my summer 'grind,' as it is affectionately termed, had prepared me for the physical rigors that military school had in store for me.

50 pushups later, I looked up at the CSM and arrogantly said, "This is easy, what else you got." He loudly yelled, telling me to get up. Next, he moved on to interrogate Kevin, the other contender of the attested "nervous laugh. *Great*, I thought, *we're all done.*

At the beginning of his interrogation, my train of thought was interrupted by yelling from a nearby field. Little did I know, a former Army Ranger and a future government employee was hollering at me.

"Cadet!" this physically fit beast yelled at me, "Have you received your haircut yet?"

I replied, "Nope..." Another huge mistake.

"Nope?" he gasped. "Nope?!! Ooooooooooo boy, you gon' learn how we do things around here, son!"

I was going to learn. In fact, that was the last time I failed to address an adult with "yes sir" or "no sir," aside from when I had permission. I'll admit, that came as a culture shock to my family, friends, and friends' parents. My mother would say, "Where is my son and what have you done with him?"

I remember when I came home my first Thanksgiving break, I called a teenager serving me at the local ice cream shop, "sir," only to look back at my friends laughing at me. Later, however, I discovered that this military-style etiquette was received with endearing glances, especially from older generations.

As soon as Kevin stuttered through a "Y-Y-Yes Command Sergeant Major," we were both laughing. Luckily, as we stood at the front of the line, we were able to quickly escape and move onto our next obstacle - the dreaded buzz cut. As we stepped in to get our heads shaved, we desperately tried to think of ways we could persuade the barber to let us keep most of our hair. We started to entertain ways to bribe her. "Oh, you look so nice today...think you could use blade three instead of one - promise not to tell," we volleyed our one-liners. "Nah," I responded, "too obvious."

As Kevin and I entered the room, our hope was squashed and we knew our fate was about to be sealed. A Chinese cadet (and my future roommate), Zhang sat slumped in the barber's seat, begging the barber to cut him some slack. However, a grisly presence ordered her to "keep doing what you're doing." I later learned this was LT Harp, the Ranger... the adult whom I had said "nope" to. My body slumped and any glimmer of hope I had came crashing down. There was no way I was going to get out of this haircut. Of course, as I feared, the barber was relentless. The haircut I walked out with was probably the worst haircut I had ever received in my life. "Hideous," I mumbled as I gazed in the mirror. I had *volunteered* for this?

The Smile of Growth

LT Harp looked at me and smiled. His smile was notoriously known around campus. Many were convinced that this smile reflected his appreciation for pain. In reality, he was smiling at "growth." This growth, as he understood it from his shortcomings and eventual success in Ranger School, was the result of sweat, tears, and venturing far outside of one's comfort zone. This smile, reminding me of the grin of demons from the movie *Insidious: The First Chapter*, made me sink in my chair. Yet, the mindset that accompanied this smile was backed by his life of self-improvement. As he inspected my new buzz cut, LT Harp asserted, "It builds character."

Whatever, I thought at the time.

He was absolutely right. Putting yourself through uncomfortable situations is the only way to build character and mental strength. LT Harp, as I would later find out, didn't have a choice in learning this. He fought and beat cancer, not once, but several times in his life. Rumor has it that when told he only had a short time to live, he trained his body with the most vigorous exercise regime disciplining both mind and body to get in line - to beat the disease. Mind over matter? Could that be what defeated his cancer? I suppose you'll just have to find out for yourself in his book.

LT Harp experienced Army Ranger School twice. He was forced to repeat a large portion of the training in order to receive his Ranger tab. If you are familiar with the Navy SEALs, the Army Rangers are the SEALs of the Army. Sleep deprivation, food deprivation, 100-pound backpack hikes, and twenty-hour-a-day physical exertion is typical at Ranger School.

Kevin and I walked out of the barber intimidated and unsettled by the masculinity of the Army Ranger Lieutenant who had directed that all our hair be cut off. Compared to him, we felt effeminate and worthless. Like him, however, we would build our worth. This worth would develop as we harnessed our military bearing, strength, work ethic, and ethos to strive for perfection in all tasks. "The worst is yet to come," quipped CSM Jim as I headed to the cadet "barracks."

The Gains

If you have any friends that lift weights as part of their daily workout repertoire, a common term you might hear repeatedly mentioned is creatine - the mysterious looking powder that supposedly "builds muscle." You might also hear your friend mention what time they woke up to lift weights. Even more, the composition of their daily protein shake. I call it "gruel." Let's not forget, the amount of weight they can bench. Finally, they flex their muscles after what they refer to as a "hardcore workout" and mention the "gains."

My parents always shared that hard situations "build character." Character 'gains' are exactly what military schools offer. However, in order to "gain" discipline, morals, personal accountability, and productivity, students must drink their daily protein shake; a shake with the ingredients of early wake up, following a structured routine, keeping a tidy and organized room and uniform, marching, exercising, and working for the team. Just like weight lifters must tear muscle fibers in order for them to rebuild, students must similarly have faith in a program which will strip them of everything before eventually building them back up.

When training formally started, I lost everything. Anything I took for granted prior to military school - all gone: my hip, glossy, long hair; my cool sporty clothing; my free time to binge on suspense thrillers; my privacy, my social media time, and phone privileges; my right to a messy, disorganized room; my right to speak during meals. Life as I once knew it was no more. What *really* bothered me, however, was the repeated barrage of reminders from the higher ranking cadets that *I was **not** entitled to those things anymore*. From now on, I was informed, I would have to *earn* back those privileges through hard work, respecting my cadet leadership, and by reading my least favorite book in the world - "The Standard."

Every day for my entire first month at the academy, I was told that I wasn't... worth... anything. Not even the dirt on the ground. I heard it at morning formation, when I first woke up, at mealtime, and as I flossed before bed each night. I couldn't put my hands on the table while eating, leave the dinner table without asking permission, or even lay on my bed until Taps - 2130 (that's 9:30 p.m. in military time). I had to talk to my Cadet Command leaders a specific way, clean my room a certain way (more than specific), and do everything at a designated time. Lastly and most challenging - no cell phone for the first month of school.

Not being permitted to speak at the dinner table allowed for time of reflection. Some days, my thoughts wandered in a negative spiral - towards quitting. I'm not sure why, but something in me kept me going. At first it seemed to be my ego keeping me in the fight. Then I surveyed my past. Up until military school, I probably had one of the strictest gymnastics coaches in the industry refer to me as"stupid boy" for almost three years. Having practice take up most of my time after school, I was left to finish my homework in the wee hours of the night. That was challenging in and of itself. My coach was hard on me, but it produced a toughness, a grit inside of me that would keep me going. I often thought about his relentless style and how far it got me. I hated him yet I loved him for it. My memories lingered to when I was a nine-year-old Taekwondo black belt. In my head, I replayed over and over that etched-in-my-brain sparring match: my opponent's rapid kick to my head.

No doubt, the stifling restrictions that Redboards had to endure were far worse than the shame of being a freshman at a public high school. Redboards were at the bottom of the food chain, and the only way to escape was to rank up. I was up for the challenge. Also, age didn't matter here. An eighth grade, high ranking student could discipline a high school student. While walking to class one day, I was in disbelief when I saw a ninth-grade sergeant command a senior redboard to do push-ups. Only at St. John's!

Being told that I didn't deserve anything was probably the best truth I ever received during my time at the school. It took me nearly a year to wholeheartedly grasp the concept. I went through the school of hard knocks, punishment brought on by yours truly. I had to learn and embrace authority and respect. Like it or not, I could no longer disrespect the higher ranking students in charge of me.

Humility and the gains didn't just come to me while

doing "iron mikes" down the guard path in a raincoat. I didn't digest humility as I ate with my back straight, my eyes forward, and my mouth closed. I couldn't smell humility as I got low in the wax of my glossy floor. I couldn't find it in accountability formations, either.

The gains came when I started soliciting my peers for help, specifically Kevin and Tommy. Humility started coming when I stopped complaining, downed my daily protein shake, and kept on. The gains came when I stopped mouthing off and accepting that I wasn't worth anything until I proved myself.

Because of my stubborn nature, what could have taken a week took over five months - my improvement emerged in baby steps. Everything I learned, I acquired the hard way.

FIVE-BABY STEPS

"First platoon outside in front of your rooms!" my cadet platoon sergeant, John Chris, yelled, "10... 9... 8... 7... 6... 5... 4... 3... 2... 1... 0!!" As platoon sergeant, John Chris was the NCO in charge of all twenty-five cadets that lived on the floor - all members of the platoon. When I say in charge, I mean *in charge.* Outside of school, we came out of our rooms when he said. We went where *he* wanted us and in the right uniform. We did the activities that he had planned. Yes, even on the weekends. This could include room inspections, shoe shining "parties," and even team-building exercises on the obstacle course.

Sergeant Chris, as I knew him, yelled at me on a regular basis. He disciplined me (mostly for my cocky attitude) almost daily. However, even when I was being disciplined... when on the verge of tears, Sergeant Chris always told me he believed in me. In doing so he influenced me. He inspired me. He was only a sophomore in high school at the time.

If I gave you a list of the names of the ten people who have influenced me the most in the last five years, that list would mainly consist of my cadet leadership at St. John's. These cadets weren't necessarily my friends, but they were my mentors.

That's what makes military school so unique: **for almost all aspects of student life, students are in charge of students and faculty supervise.** Not just any faculty, however. We are entrusted to faculty who have served in the military - faculty who understand a thing or two about leadership.

My platoon shuffled into the hallway. It was 0630. Wakeup call. The sound of reveille echoing across campus from loudspeakers was quickly dampened by the yawning in the hallway, and then interrupted by my squad leader - Corporal Din. "You're late, cadet Porter! Fix yourself!" he admonished. Like me, Porter must have had trouble waking up, jumping off the top bunk, putting on shoes, and getting into the hallway in only ten seconds. I smirked at my roommate, Tommy, who stood on the other side of the door, facing the center of the hallway. After initial morning roll call, room inspections took place.

On the third day of school, Tommy and I had become accustomed to the standards and "tricks" to make our room pass inspection on a day-to-day basis. We knew that black socks and underwear went in the second drawer, that hospital corners on our beds needed to be at forty-five degree angles, and that books on the shelf must descend from tallest to shortest from right to left. Tommy also was a prior gymnast. Like me, he too paid attention to detail, a quality which made us shine during room inspections. Ironically, Tommy also had trained under a Russian coach. He knew the drill.

We had a superior room. Most likely the best on the floor. Later in the school-year, when we eventually used our clean room as an excuse to fly under the radar in the mornings, Squad Leader Din, a hard working cadet from Korea, saw right through our ploy of "getting by."

One morning, Din barged into our room, slammed the door shut, and proceeded to inspect our room. Glancing behind me into the room to see what he was doing, I was blindsided. I was given the order to do push-ups. "Front leaning rest, Chauff," I heard for the first time this morning, yet probably the hundredth time this year. In a smart alec, clueless tone, the words escaped my mouth, "But I didn't even do anything."

Sergeant Chris came into the room. "Earlier, you looked around during my inspection, now get down and do 20 pushups."

Silly as it sounds, there was no looking around during inspections. That was a major violation.

I got down into my all too familiar push-up position. Tommy looked down at me and smirked. Typical Tommy. As soon as Sergeant Chris returned to our side of the hallway, Tommy did what we all did when laughing during inspection - play it off as a cough. Leadership had already caught on, and the situation escalated from bad to worse. Next thing I knew, three different squad leaders appeared out of nowhere standing in my room, joining Din in the hopes of finding some other offense. To take their place in the hallway, three squad leaders from the downstairs platoon surged up the dated and worn stairwell to remind us why the two of us as deserved pushups.

There were more offenses. My square corners, as my squad leader said, were "ten degrees off." My books were "not flush against the edge of the shelf." But the way that Din expressed this made Tommy and I burst out into laughter. "The bed is wong! Fix yo woom! Book on edge! Forty figh Degwee!"

You didn't make fun of people at St. John's... it was just a conviction we all knew or eventually developed... especially not the leaders. The only higher form of disrespect was stepping on the school crest - an act punishable by doing one pushup for each year since its inception - then 132.

Next thing I knew, my bed was on the ground, my closet was busted open for further inspection, and the clothing in my drawers was thrown onto the desk. I was in for what was affectionately termed, a "bed making party."

The lucky participants of a bed making party have two minutes to make their beds. At the end of the two minutes, the party "host," Din in this case, would inspect the beds. If any of the beds didn't pass the inspection, both would be ripped apart and the party would resume once again.

Why did they make Tommy do it? Because we were what the military calls "battle buddies." We were a two man team that **owned** our room. If I failed, it was just as much his fault as it was mine. The same was true for me if he failed. I was usually the one that messed up, the one who got him in trouble for laughing, and the one whose side of the room was disheveled.

Forget the bed making party. I found it outrageous that I could get penalized for things that he did! He probably thought the same. However, a "team" mentality was birthed by the academy and, as ludicrous as it seemed, taught me accountability. It taught me to look beyond my own immature, short sighted feelings and work *for* my battle buddy. When I entered leadership, my freshman, sophomore, junior, and senior years, I began to work *for* the squad I was leading, *for* the company I was leading, *for* the tutors I was leading, and eventually *for* the 136th Corps of Cadets. The notion of working *for* others instead of for myself became a healthy pressure. **It is under this type of pressure that a military style institution works - the metamorphosis of young boys and girls into the leaders of tomorrow is achieved.**

I didn't care about the "team," I thought to myself while making the bed Din would tear apart anyways. I felt bad for Tommy, whose face was stop-sign red, seething with anger. That was never good.

After ten attempts, Tommy and I were exhausted. Our hands reeked of a combined smell - a potion of sweat and wool lint. Silence. You could cut the tension with a knife. Not only were we becoming aggravated with each other, but we felt deep resentment for our squad leader, who seemed unphased with our repeated attempts. Finally, we passed the inspection. That was the last time I ever made my bed anything short of perfect.

The room inspections and bed-making parties seemed cruel and unnecessary. They were the icing on the military cake for my first year in school. Yet, they served a higher purpose than just teaching me how to make a bed or scrub a floor. They taught me to strive for discipline and detail oriented thinking - two valuable qualities which I now believe are characteristic of those claiming to be successful. I gained the discipline to clean a room to perfection every day, but also realized the attention to detail that comes with doing things the right way, the first time. That's something worth repeating.

Doing things exactly right, the first time.

That can be applied to every single aspect of one's life. For example, doing the math homework **exactly right the first time**. Doing the dishes **exactly right the first time.** Filling out the report for the boss **exactly right the first time**. Cutting corners, something that people today tend to do more than anytime in history, is the antithesis of doing things exactly right, the first time.

A series of small lessons like this transformed me from the insecure, immature, and smug eighth grader into the confident, mature, humble young man I aspire to be today. That's at least what my friends, parents, and yes, my previous babysitters, tell me. I know not everyone has the desire to endure military-style training in order to mature. Honestly, if I knew the full scope of what I was getting into, I would have declined the opportunity. That's where my role as the author comes in. I want to give you, the reader, a roadmap and picture of a few of the lessons I learned in military school. A roadmap that just might lead you on the right path to the summit. Close your eyes and envision it...

So You're Serious

There are so many things I want to express. There are things I would like to explain to you that go far beyond the scope of this book. I wish I could sit in a room with you and tell you *everything* that I've learned thus far.

Since you're clearly serious about reading this book, I want you to consider this. The Pew Research Center came out with a study in 2015 which concluded that around one in four American adults have not read a book in the last year. That's a shame considering that America is the most resourceful country on the face of the earth.

Since **you *are* reading this book and *are* seeking to improve**, I would say that you're already ahead of about 25% of your competition, around 64 million adults. We just need to get you past the other 75%.

If you're not concerned with personal development, then perhaps stop reading. You've got my story and by now my stories have grown tiresome. Beyond this point, this book is solely a roadmap for you... for your growth... for your future. Don't fret, you're still going to continue to hear a few of my cringeworthy moments. However, the premise of the next section of this book is solely about you. As you read, I encourage you to apply the lessons learned to your life. Have something to take notes with. Have you read something funny? **Write it down.** Has something inspired you? **Write it down.**

The Other 75%

In order for you to get you ahead of the other 75% of people, I'll encourage you to start your journey, or get back onto your line. However, I have to let you in on a little secret. This is a secret I've come across after major heartache and disappointment. Becoming happier, smarter, more productive, and going wherever you want to go in life is not something that you can attain by changing the environment around you. Reading and applying the lessons from countless self-help books and memoirs of the successful has led me to one conclusion. **90% of your journey to becoming successful, happy, or anything you want to become depends on you changing yourself.**

Things to change might include your attitude, work ethic, self image, the way you interact with others, and more. On this journey, you should assume that the environment you are living in is a constant, and that *you* are the variable that needs to change. When you change your mindset, make smarter decisions, and change yourself, then the environment around you will follow suit.

So many people think that the problems in their life stem from the environment around them. They blame their life situation on their parents, their boss, previous relationships, or even God. Here's something I know. The biggest problem in my life, is me. The biggest problem in your life, is you. How do we fix our biggest problem? We get in front of the mirror and we look inside. As we embark further on this journey, we'll find that when we focus on our 90% of the deal and keep our end of the 90% regardless of the circumstances, the other 10% works itself out.

The name of the game is making your side of the "deal" so consolidated, focused, and well put together that nothing in the other 10% that life throws at you can break you. It's realizing that you need to control *your* 90%, not becoming anxious about the other 10%. That's a leap that only the people who desire success the most can make.

David Goggins, Navy SEAL and Ultramarathon runner, has had a huge impact on my life. When asked in an interview why he ran so much even though he hated running, Goggins responded:

> *"By me running, I am callusing my mind. I'm not training for a race, I'm training for life. I'm training for the time when I get that two o'clock in the morning call that my mom is dead or something happens tragic in my life, [so that] I don't fall apart. I'm training my mind and my body and my spirit so it's all one so I can handle what life is going to throw at me."*

Goggins is known as the "toughest man on the face of the earth." He makes the leap to control his 90% of the battle daily.

He does this through extreme exercise and hard work. Attacking his 90% of the deal has made him an amazing individual - one oblivious to the other 10%. Don't worry, you'll hear about Goggins again in the pages to come.

Any of us can make that leap. We just need a platform to stand on. A platform of confidence and discipline. Military school and my mistakes built my platform. It's my goal to build it for yourself.

The Deal

Our 90%
Our mindset, our attitude, our effort given, our care factor, our words, our actions, our decisions, our desire to learn and improve, our good and bad habits, our overall organization, our values, our self image, how we treat others.

The Other 10%
Luck, actions of others, opportunities presented to us, accidents, sickness, natural disasters.

Dealing With Correction

Sorry to break it to you, but I can't build your platform for you. Well, I can... sort of. I know you want to build a platform that won't break - a stable one from which you can make your jump. How about a steel platform with a well-constructed ladder? Well, all I can really do is bring you to the toolshed and show you where the tools are. The people that can teach you how to use the tools are your authorities: parents, coaches, teachers, doctors, etc. You don't want to use tools? Just try ignoring your authorities and making a platform out of mud or sand. I tried it in middle school - evidently it didn't work. As you know, things only got worse.

I want to address the concept of authority - the people in your life with the experience and instructions on how you can make your personalized, top of the line platform. You probably don't like every person in your life that is "in charge" of you. Think back to when you ever had a coach, family member, or teacher that was hard on you. Were they a Russian gymnastics coach? A math tutor? A little league soccer coach? Did it seem like they always had something negative to say about your performance? "You're not working hard enough," they might have told you, "Start putting some actual effort into that soccer kick!" I find that it's so easy to just disregard those types of authority figures. I used to regard them as irritable, mean, or just unhappy people who didn't really want to help me.

Just the opposite is true. **The people that are the hardest on you are usually the people who truly want to see you succeed.** I didn't understand this until I spoke with my Russian coach for the last time. With tears in his eyes, he told me that I was probably the hardest working gymnast he ever worked with. He told me that I had been a "good boy." These were the only two complements he ever gave me.

For years, I perceived his correction as relentless criticism to get me to quit the sport. He pushed and pushed me. After all, I was the worst gymnast on the team. On the contrary, all the times he told me to point my toes, straighten my back, and stop being a "stupid boy" - it was all to create a better me. Had I conceptualized that earlier, perhaps I would have been a better gymnast and even have placed higher at competitions. Who was the loser here?

Now think back to who the last "tough authority" was for you. Think about how much more wisdom, knowledge, and experience they had in the field than you. There are three ways you could have responded to this authority when corrected:

1. With attitude and disrespect.
2. With respectful acknowledgement but without true application of their correction.

3. With deep reverence and quick application of the authority's correction.

Everyone has given the first response to their parents at some point. if you're honest with yourself, you'll come to realize how much energy this robs you of. It's exhausting to argue and debate! Arguing only perpetuates the issue leaving you depressed and despondent. Likewise, the same occurs when you respond similarly to anyone over you. Responding with a rebellious attitude not only makes you look second-rate, it makes you less likely to succeed.

The second response is almost as bad (I dare say that it's even worse). You acknowledge the authority's correction, but disregard it. You politely nod your head, but inwardly you dismiss the direction because you believe that your ability level is superior. What stands between you and your authority? Is it a wall of pride? Could this be the culprit and the dividing characteristic of the haves and the have nots of professional sports? I've often wondered if more greatness could have been achieved with the dismantling of this pride.

What I've found is that the people who respond to those "in charge" of them in the third way, listening to what's being said and then applying it, are those who usually end up becoming authorities themselves. These are the most characteristically humble people, who potentially rise to the top. In the end, they learn the most from their moody physics teacher, their drill sergeant soccer coach, and follow the advice that their parents so liberally dole out to them. They gain by losing any form of pride.

"True strength lies in submission which permits one to dedicate his life, through devotion, to something beyond himself." - Henry Miller

Thinking back, what if you had followed all the advice

and or direction given to you by those "over you." Hmmmmm... is it possible your outcome could be very different today? Where and what would you be? My conviction is that you'd probably be much more mature, happier, and overall living somewhat of a better life.

Listen to your authorities and do as they say, regardless of whether you want to or not. You'll find yourself less stressed and learning beyond your imagination. When those over you notice your transformed attitude, they will gravitate toward helping you even more. Had I known this, I would have avoided an obscene amount of pushups during my first year at military school.

So if You Want to Change the World...

You can probably guess by now how I spend my first two minutes of every morning - I make my bed. But I don't just "make" my bed. I craft my bed just like my squad leader taught me - to utmost perfection. It's now in my subconscious, something I don't even think about anymore. Although it may seem small, making my bed is one of the most important things military school ingrained in me. Even in the event of a bad day, I could come back to my perfectly made bed knowing that I had completed something worthwhile that day.

Retired Navy SEAL Admiral McRaven, in his University of Texas Commencement Speech, explains how when a person makes their bed, they are able to "accomplish the first task of the day," therefore boosting their worth and motivation in order to complete further tasks throughout the day. As he so eloquently stated, making one's bed "reinforces the fact that the little things in life matter. If you can't do the little things right, you will never be able to do the big things right."

Admiral McRaven's speech is definitely worth watching. His clear and simple message at the end of his speech got my attention. "So if you want to change the world, start off by making your bed."

Newton's first law of motion states that an object at rest stays at rest and an object in motion stays in motion. Sometimes, on the off days when you *really* don't want to go to the gym or finish up that assignment, making your bed is the activity that puts you "in motion." There's something about looking at the crispness of your bed after you make it that gives you confidence and makes you *want* to get more done. Just try it!

Envision the top CEO's, businessmen, and other leaders of the world. Many of them, as you can already guess, make their bed. Unfortunately, the rest of America does not follow suit. Though wanting to understand the secret to their icon's success, this particular routine is just simply overlooked. According to *today.yougov.com*, a study of 4,110 United States adults showed that only 37% of Americans habitually make their beds. Further findings suggest that older people, assumed to be more disciplined and well-versed, make their beds more regularly than younger people. The same study reported 47% of individuals aged 55 and older regularly made their beds, compared to 31% of those aged 18-24. I find that to be interesting. There *is* a correlation between discipline and making your bed.

Stubborn Fool #3

At age thirteen, this stubborn fool lived with his family in a rented room within the house. His dream was to be a singer. Thus, at eighteen years of age, he walked into a record company with a demo disk in hand. Twice the record was disregarded. He then auditioned to become part of a music group and was rejected. He was told, in not so many words, that he "couldn't sing." He resorted to driving a truck for a living. During his time as a truck driver, he met a man named Eddie Bond, who led a professional band. The man who "couldn't sing," interestingly enough, was Elvis Presley. He went on to sell one billion records worldwide. That would make him one of the most popular musicians that ever walked the face of the earth.

So who's telling you that you "can't sing?" Somebody in your life is probably doubting that you can do something. Let them doubt you. It's all white noise. Think about how awesome it would be to pull an Elvis Presley in your current situation. **Now transfer those thoughts into action.**

Falling Behind

You're falling behind in your work. On Wednesday afternoon, you observe the mountain of assignments and the dread of tackling them. The to-do's and commitments you have to satisfy in order to make it through Thursday and Friday give you heartburn. You pledge allegiance to productivity *over the weekend* in order to get ahead for the next week. However, when Friday evening approaches, you are tempted to do absolutely nothing. Although you know what needs to be done over the weekend, your Friday and Saturday often end up on the couch, wrapped in a blanket, watching Netflix, consuming a vast amount of potato chips.

You wake up on Sunday - it's "grind it out" time. Out of the corner of your productive eye, you notice the pile of work only getting higher. You are behind and realize you should have put in the work last week. When you get started on to-do #1 of 14, you quickly lose enthusiasm and motivation. If you didn't have a to-do list, you'd be even worse off. Because you can't see yourself getting the unrealistic amount of work done, you further procrastinate, avoid your desk, or focus on the to-do's that aren't high on the priority list. With that, you decide to "take the day off" and resume again on Monday. When Monday rolls around, your to-do list is now 18 tasks long. Because you know you cannot possibly get everything done, you choose to avoid the tasks that can be "strategically" dismissed. Your self confidence takes a huge hit. You then pledge to never procrastinate again. This becomes a vicious cycle, week after week, month after month, and you miss opportunity after opportunity. Each time you "pledge" to get your laundry list of to-do's done and procrastinate or just don't do them, you lower your self confidence. You start to believe that something is wrong with you, or that working hard just "isn't for you." Then you entertain thoughts of giving up. You get the point.

Let's be honest. We've all written an essay for a class the night before or the day of. We've all fallen victim to the silent killer of procrastination - the #1 business destroyer. The factor that lowered our grade point average the most. The biggest time vacuum of our day.

To tackle this problem, I read the book *Organize Tomorrow Today*. Authors Jason Selk and Tom Bartow gave advice that I didn't expect - advice for **achieving more by doing less**. Their advice was revolutionary. Selk and Bartow, in their years of helping Olympic-level athletes and business CEO's develop mental toughness, discovered that "Highly successful people never get it all done in any one given day - but they always get the most important things done each day."

Getting the most important things accomplished doesn't mean writing out all thirty to-do's on a single sheet. It is not waking up at 4:00 a.m. and doing one and a half hours of cardio training before starting work. It most certainly does not include a complex diet, regimented sleep schedule, or legalistic meditation regiment.

The key is prioritization. Selk and Bartlow's extremely effective, simple method to prioritizing tasks consists of making a "three most important" list. Usually made the night before, the "three most important" list includes the three highest in priority tasks that need to be completed first and foremost in the day. Not fourteen tasks. Not seven tasks. Not four easy tasks that you enjoy doing, but rather the three, highest priority tasks. It's ingenious!! Written next to these three specific tasks is the time by which the tasks should be completed. Taking even higher priority than the "Three Most Important" list is the "one must." This is the one task out of your three that will be *the* highest priority task you complete that day. It is to be done first. My first list looked something like this:

1.Finish Detailed Outline for History Essay	8 a.m.
2.Complete Triangles Geometry Homework	9 a.m.
3.Complete 2 practice ACT Science Tests	10:30 a.m.

By 10:30 a.m., I had completed the three most important tasks that pertained to my day (besides making my bed). Not only that, I adhered to the schedule I made for myself. By nature, I tend to lean toward a cynical perspective; I see the glass half empty so to speak. Accomplishing the tasks at hand rather than putting them off was the start of a habit that greatly boosted my confidence. Completing my three most important tasks gave me even *more* momentum. I was on a mission now, and the other tasks would be a piece of cake!

I recommend, one Saturday or Sunday, waking up 30 minutes earlier than you normally would. Mentally prepare the night before and make a list of what needs to be done. Oh, and don't forget to include making your bed. Yes, it is a priority.

Next, select your top three tasks at hand. Write them on a notecard or a note card-sized piece of paper in the "three most important" format. Actually follow your own schedule - to the "T." Don't worry about the results! Just focus on following the process that you made for yourself. Most importantly, do not forget to **cross off completed tasks**. Making progress feels… so… good. In his article Micro-Tasks. The Pleasure of Checking Off, Francisco Sáez explains the neurological explanation for the "feel good" of completing a task.

> *"Whenever you recognize a task or project as completed, your brain releases a good amount of dopamine, a neuro-*

transmitter that is responsible for generating feelings of accomplishment, satisfaction and joy. This release of dopamine not only makes you feel good but also motivates you to continue completing tasks, thus prolonging that 'pleasant feeling.'"

One Bite at a Time

William approached me the night before his four page research paper was due. His hands were clammy, his face was red; he was riddled with anxiety - the prime symptoms of procrastination. In my EMT class, we would say he was showing early stages of shock. "You need to help me get this done Chauff," William sulked, "I just can't focus."

He handed me his computer along with a blank document staring back at me. I turned down the brightness and frowned. "Start by putting your name, the class, the teacher's name, and the date in the upper left hand corner of this document," I said as I handed back his computer.

He sat down at my desk and complied. He soon handed me back his computer.

I leaned back in my chair. "The essay is due tomorrow. The current time is 5:00 p.m. Lights out at 10:00 p.m. That leaves you with roughly four to five hours to cram."

His eyes looked down in disappointment. "So you're not going to write my essay for me?"

Word around campus my sophomore year was that I did cadets' essays for them. Truth be told, I just showed them how to get the job done.

"Absolutely not. But I'll tell you this. You *will* get this essay done, you *will* get a passing grade, and you *will* get to bed by 10:00 p.m. Let me show you how." I was amazed at what I heard come out of my mouth, escaping my lips before I could put a reign on my tongue.

William glared at me with disbelief. After some time, he sunk into my chair with a sigh of relief. "Thank you, Chauff. Okay, I'll just start writing right now."

"Stop!!" I grabbed the computer with one hand. "How do you eat an elephant...." he cut me off.

"One bite at a time."

William would be enjoying a several-course meal for dinner tonight, and he didn't know where to begin. Therein lied the problem.

William aggressively pounced on his research paper from ground zero. It was the equivalent of shoving mashed potatoes, filet mignon, wine, salad, and jumbo shrimp all in his mouth simultaneously. Picture sticking a fork in an elephant and trying to maneuver it into his mouth - it just wouldn't work. So William and I broke down his meal into five parts: drinks (research), appetizers (outline), entree #1 (writing the essay), entree #2 (revising the essay), and dessert (works cited). Together, we broke those down into even smaller, bite-sized parts. In doing so, William had twenty specific bites to finish his meal. Now that's more tolerable. Below is the exact outline I made for him.

Part 1 - Research (50 minutes total)
A) 6 bullet points from source 1 on topic A (10 minutes)
B) 6 bullet points from source 2 on topic B (10 minutes)
C) 6 bullet points from source 3 on topic C (10 minutes)
D) 6 bullet points from source 3 on topic D (10 minutes)
E) 3 quotes from source 4 on topic E (10 minutes)

Part 2 - Outline (50 minutes total)
A) Introduction and hook statement (5 minutes)
B) Body Paragraph 1 (10 minutes)
C) Body Paragraph 2 (10 minutes)
D) Body Paragraph 3 (10 minutes)
E) Body Paragraph 4 (10 minutes)
F) Conclusion (5 minutes)

Part 3 - Writing the essay (50 minutes total)
A) Introduction (5 minutes)
B) Body Paragraph 1 (10 minutes)
C) Body Paragraph 2 (10 minutes)
D) Body Paragraph 3 (10 minutes)
E) Body Paragraph 4 (10 minutes)
F) Conclusion (5 minutes)

Part 4 - Revising the essay (30 minutes total)
A) Read through #1 (10 minutes)
B) Read through #2 (10 minutes)
C) Final Read through (10 minutes)

Part 5 - Works Cited (15 minutes total)

That schedule gave William around three hours and thirty minutes to knock out his essay (remember, at this late stage of the game we just wanted him to get a *passing* grade). When we broke the task down, William was easily able to finish the process, with time to spare. Even though he found one of the articles to be extremely fascinating and was later tempted to check his snapchat, I forcefully had to redirect him to stay on schedule. William received a C+ on his paper. He was content.

The point of this lesson is to emphasize that **breaking tasks into smaller subtasks is the best way to actually tackle them.** What if William, when he received the assignment a week before the due date, would have created what I call the **Elephant Bite Outline** (EBO)? In an EBO, you write down any task you need to accomplish, you split it up into "bite-sized" pieces, and you give a time estimate for how long it will take you to "eat" each piece, as demonstrated earlier.

With the EBO, William could have spent 50 minutes a day working on his essay and finishing it before Friday. The result: a stress-free weekend.

At military school, the day is extremely structured. Some days are busier than others. On those packed days I would find myself with only a few twenty minute blocks of free time between activities, such as between breakfast and first-period. I have several EBO in a folder on my desk at all times. At any given time, I take out one of my EBO's and take a quick bite off of one of my major tasks, or Elephants. Junior year, my Elephants included preparing for the ACT, organizing and spearheading a tutoring program, and writing this book, on top of other assigned projects and schoolwork. Using the EBO was how I was able to write this book, a majority of which was written during the 30-minute interim after breakfast and before my first period class.

If you can train yourself to systematically break your tasks into bite-sized pieces and consistently "eat" them one by one, you will find yourself getting more work done than ever before. You'll also be less intimidated by that mountainous, taunting project because you've broken it down into manageable tasks.

With food, the more the intake, the larger your waist size becomes. When it comes to success, the more bites you take (the more action you take), the closer you get to finishing the elephant and the more successful you become. Another way to look at this is with a staircase analogy. You're at the bottom of a flight of stairs. At the top of those stairs is that what you want, be it money, success, a goal of yours, or the six pack abs you've always dreamed of. Getting to the top of the stairs is not done in a single step. Taking too many steps at one time leads to burnout, and not taking any steps leads to procrastination, to no progress, and finally to no success. Getting to the top of the steps is the result of **consistent** effort. Understand that the most triumphant people are not those with the highest IQ's! They are simply those who A - **Figure out what is at the top of the stairs**, B - **Find the stairs**, and C - **Walk straight up**. Successful people are those who, regardless of the consequences, the grit, or the sacrifices necessary, are willing to take that first step. As Charles J. Givens so matter of factly stated, "Success requires first expending ten units of effort to produce one unit of results. Your momentum will then produce ten units of results with each unit of effort."

What these people have in common - entrepreneurs, olympic athletes, marathon runners - they all understand that you can't be thinking about stair eight when you are only on stair one. In whatever task you seek to accomplish, you must **focus and give full attention to the current step**.

So let me lay it out for you once and for all. This is how you can systematically attack any task, goal, objective, ambition, or anything.

Step 1: Define what it is exactly at the top of the stairs that you desire.

Is it one million dollars? Is it a Fortune 500 company? Is it a raise? A promotion? Is it an A on a math test? Is it completing a history essay? Make it clear.

Step 2: Know your staircase and find it.

Regardless of what is at the top of the staircase, you first need to evaluate it. Isolate and break down the task into subtasks and estimate how much time each mini-task will take. Remember, without stairs, you will never get very far. As Zig Ziglar so famously stated, "there is no elevator to success... you have to take the stairs."

Step 3: Focus on one step at a time on your way to the top of the stairs.

This is the most important step to accomplishing anything. Without this piece of advice, you will never accomplish anything at your full potential. Scary. **You have to give undivided attention to each step as you climb.** Is your goal to get through Navy SEAL BUDs training? Most Navy SEALs would tell you to focus on giving full effort to just get to the next meal. Is your goal to write a book? Try writing a certain amount of words a day. Do you want to be a physician? First focus on getting a good GPA in college or studying for the MCAT. Do you want to run 26.2 miles? Start with just running two miles and add a mile each week.

It's a start. Remember, some don't even get *that* far.

"The only place success comes before work is in the dictionary." - Vince Lombardi

❖ ❖ ❖

Stubborn Fool #4

He was 65 years old and on the verge of poverty. His restaurant was at best mediocre. Once retired, he focused on sharing his fried chicken recipe. In his town, he went door to door, house to house, restaurant to restaurant. When this produced little results, he started traveling by car to institutions he hoped would sell his chicken. Before his recipe was accepted, he was turned down 1,009 times. Once accepted, Colonel Harland Sanders' chicken was highly coveted. If it wasn't for his undeniable efforts, Kentucky Fried Chicken would not be here today.

Sanders' story defines inspiration. The amount of dedication and persistence needed to overlook over 1,000 rejections is both admirable and worthy of imitation.

Now consider the words of Joyce Meyer. "I wonder how many times people give up just before a breakthrough - when they are on the very brink of success."

The Slime

The "fight-or-flight response" is the body's way to prepare to either react or retreat. When in the presence of harmful stimuli or certain chemicals, receptors and sections of the brain will prime the body to either take action or flee. During such a response, the heart rate increases, blood sugar increases, breaths shorten, and of course, the brain signals stress. Think of how a boxer feels before a big match - "hyped up," extremely nervous, and only focused on one thing: the upcoming fight.

In today's society, our minds will occasionally take seemingly normal situations and convert them into "fight or flight" reactions. Upcoming deadlines, awkward social interactions, anticipated final's week, and public speaking can become our worst nightmares. The fear in our minds will often compel us to avoid these situations or worse yet, paralyze us amidst them.

My conviction? It is good to be nervous about upcoming events. Pressure can be helpful for increasing performance. Entertaining thoughts that paralyze us, however, is not okay. I call this phenomenon **the slime**.

Adar showed up at my door on a Tuesday. He had essays, projects, and finals for the rest of the week. I could see the panic in his eyes along with his body language expressing angst. He didn't know how he was going to get everything done. "I just have so much that I need to get done!!" he cried, "Chauff! I don't know what to do!! I've got Spanish and History and my English newspaper project and counseling forms and Trigonometry and I just want to give up!!!" As Adar sat in my black chair, his hands fidgeted, his legs nervously shook, and his eyes remained wide in disbelief.

Adar was in **the slime**. He was so anxious to get everything done on time that he was overtaken and frozen with fear. In this situation, "fight or flight" was preventing him from taking action. In his head, "fighting" the situation, regardless of how much effort was expended, would lead to destruction. So, his mind was choosing flight.

Adar sat on my bed. I told him that he needed to take a proverbial deep breath. It was obvious how stressed out he was about his finals. However, he was stuck in the slime and couldn't take action. Again, much like William, he didn't know where to

begin. So I asked Adar to close his eyes and tell me everything he needed to complete throughout the week (and how long each task would take). The list I wrote down for him looked something like this:
- English Final (4 hours)
- Spanish Final (2 hours)
- History Final (2 hours)
- English project (5 hours)
- Cadet counseling form (30 minutes)
- Trigonometry worksheets (1.5 hours)

Adar was surprised when he saw that he only had 15 hours of homework. He had convinced himself that it was over 100 hours of work.

When you're overwhelmed like Adar, I encourage you to write everything needed to be accomplished down on paper. There's something about visualizing the pressing tasks instigating this "overwhelming" feeling. Somehow, it's not as mountainous as our minds trick us into thinking.

All of us have problems, upcoming deadlines, and things we need to be working on. Often times, we choose "flight" rather than fight. We flee the gym instead of fighting through a thirty-minute chest workout. We flee to our friend's house instead of tackling that essay due in a week. We flee from the library because we don't like reading. We need to choose fighting or addressing our problems rather than fleeing from them. **With some things, it's imperative you make a conscious decision to fight.**

Colonel Harland Sanders could have chosen flight over fight to get his chicken in restaurants. Thomas Edison could have chosen flight over constantly fighting to invent. Albert Einstein could have chosen flight from his critical peers over fighting for his pursuit of knowledge.

Fighting instead of fleeing is the difference between every successful person and every mediocre person. **Every successful person is a mediocre person who fought.**

SIX-BREAKTHROUGH

As I scrolled through Instagram under the protection of my thick, wool, St. John's - labeled blanket, it seemed as if I was missing out on "life." In one Instagram post, my friends from back home were living it up at an eighth-grade party. I looked up to check the door, making sure the night guard didn't catch me on my phone. "No guard, we're good, Tommy," I whispered, feeling like an undercover agent.

"Sounds good, bro. You take the look-out for another five minutes, and we'll switch at 2230."

"What time is that again?" I murmured. I didn't figure out military time until the end of my first year, after being repeatedly scolded for showing up two hours early and sometimes two hours late for mandatory functions.

"It's ten-thirty, goofball. Aren't you supposed to be smart?"

I laughed. "Not really."

"Not gonna lie, Chauff, you've probably got the street smarts of a ten-year-old child." he chuckled, "But keep me covered. I'm texting my mom."

Getting called by my last name took some acclimation. My leadership showed me that there are apparently eight different ways one can pronounce my last name: Choof, Chau, Cha, Shauff, Shoof, Shau, Chof, and Chuff.

"That's what they all say," I snickered. "But sounds good, I'll keep us covered."

Keeping watch was necessary, especially after lights out: 10:00 p.m. We had just received our phones back a few weeks ago after new-cadet training finished. We couldn't risk losing them again. Usually, Tommy and I switched out watching for the guard every ten minutes.

Carefully hiding my phone under my blanket, I resumed perusing my Instagram account. I scrolled down. In another post I stumbled upon, I saw my friends posing carefree with a group of girls sporting their Halloween costumes. On Halloween, I remembered posing at attention in my blue shirt, blue pants, and glossy, low quarters at the lowering of the flag. Forget growth, improvement, training, and maturity, I felt like I was missing out. Truth be known, Tommy and I were each other's soundboards. Without him to talk to each night, I wouldn't have been able to see past my woes of "missing out." He was my gymnastics comrade, the person I joked with at formation, and, like a lost puppy dog, the person I followed around — basically my older brother. The reality was, my friendship with Tommy, my roommate for two months, was already closer than most of my bonds back home; I didn't realize that until after Tommy left the Academy. Nonetheless, I was jealous that my friends were enjoying middle school and that I was, in my eyes, suffering in my dorm room.

It was 10:35 P.M. - apparently 2035. When I looked up above my bedsheets, I was blinded by blue light, a light very familiar to me. All I heard was a "click" before the night security officer was at the side of my bed: top bunk. He had caught my roommate and me on our phones. It was the third time this week, and we knew what that meant. We reluctantly handed over our phones. With a stern tone, the night security officer gave us both instructions:

You have two minutes to head outside to the guard path (the quad) in your raincoats and boots. Here, you will wait for further instructions. Do not be late.

As I quickly laced my boots and threw on my heavy, black raincoat, I thought back to a night 12 months earlier when my mom had caught me on my phone at an ungodly hour. "Skyler, it's almost three in the morning... what are you doing on your phone?!" my mom asked me through thick darkness and glaring disbelief.

I answered with the typical teenage attitude, "I'm just talking to my friends, chill out, Mom." I lied. I had been snapchatting with my girlfriend for five hours.

My dad walked in, and I gave him the same unapologetic response. "You can't BS a BS'er," he hollered, swiftly coming over and snatching my phone right from under me. At this point, my undeveloped seventh-grade mind had decided that arguing with my parents was a lost cause. I nonetheless enjoyed the fight - after all, it was a worthy cause to fight! They grounded me for two weeks.

I had an issue with disrespect and authority. Tommy had a problem with anger. It wasn't uncommon for him to slam doors loud enough to wake up our entire platoon. "I thought you had me covered!" Tommy gasped.

"It was your turn, man," I told him in the hallway.

"Whatever, man."

That was how it was with Tommy and I. Like brothers, we got into senseless arguments. Within minutes, however, these arguments were over, and it was like nothing ever happened - never a harbored grudge.

Opening the door of the barracks, I felt water-boarded by the rain. Only able to see three feet in front of us, Tommy and I stuck close together as we made our way to the center of the guard path. There, our NCO leadership and plight were awaiting us.

Through the rain, I caught a glimpse of two other familiar faces: Zhang and Porter. Zhang had his usual black water bottle and Porter was wearing my seventh-grade attitude of "Why am

I here, this is dumb." Zhang, a cadet from China, would be my future roommate. His transition to academy life was as smooth as rocks. While I clung to my phone for an escape from the long and stressful days, Zhang's escape was in his 15-inch, water purifying, tea making water bottle. I couldn't understand why he brought it everywhere with him: outside formation, class, and even the bathroom. It was his "baby-friend." When we first met, I curiously asked him why he carried it with him everywhere he went. "Good water," he responded with an excited smile.

Porter, a student from the Chicago suburbs like myself, was extremely bright. Porter could read anything and remember it forever. While I spent my weekends studying for a biology test, he could relax. He would usually outperform me, too. One of the things we had in common was our attitude problem. Porter also had a glaring issue with Cadet Command. He and I both competed for the most push-ups our first year; I won, but he sure was a close second. He always seemed to be on the phone "with his parents." Nothing nor anybody could interrupt that coveted time on the phone with his folks - not even room inspections. Academic performance was the one thing that could compete for his attention. GPA, as far as he was concerned, was equivalent to rank. Porter somehow was privy to everyone's GPA down to the decimal. If a squad leader fared below a 3.0, Porter played the deaf man - you might have gotten a better response from talking to a wall.

Zhang, Tommy, Porter, and I linked arms. Three squad leaders told us to start doing "iron mikes," or lunges in unison. Zhang set down his water bottle, and we began. The rain was relentless, coming down even harder as we continued.

Getting through the sharp pain of each lunge was grueling. It was not worth the time I spent on Instagram. At first, we didn't do lunges in unison (even though our arms were locked), and it made us tired, worn out, and just demoralized. Zhang's elbow somehow kept jabbing into my stomach and Porter kept stepping on my shoes. I could feel Tommy getting annoyed with Zhang for also jabbing him in the stomach. It was in the 55-degree pouring rain, when my legs were failing me, that I decided to flip the situation.

"Come on, guys, let's do this together," I murmured so that the nearby leadership wouldn't see me talking. We started lunging in unison. We were really in this together - if one of us fell, then all of us went down together. By the looks of it, Zhang and Porter were pretty close to going down. It wasn't just about me making through this, but rather about making sure we all got through this. I then realized that it was only four of us in the rain. The leadership was gone.

I decided to flip the situation further. I started yelling out "one" on our left lunges and "two" on our right. First, Tommy joined, then Porter, and finally, Zhang. "One, two, one, two!!!" we yelled at the top of our lungs for what seemed like a glorious ten minutes of lunges. The counting made us go faster. It appeared that the louder we yelled, the more energy we had. When my voice cracked, we all started laughing. We were two cadets from Chicago, a cadet from Texas, and a cadet from Beijing. In the cold rain, while doing lunges, we were yelling and laughing with and at each other on the guard path. It was a moment I'll never forget - something out of a movie. Only this wasn't a movie. This was a checkpoint on my journey now.

In the grit of the lunges, I figured something out. It's something that so many solo hikers don't figure out until it's too late. Not to sound cliche, but I learned that united forces could accomplish almost anything. The four of us couldn't see nine feet in front of us, we couldn't feel our legs, but we knew we had each other, and we kept going. Perhaps we didn't want to let the rest of the group down, or maybe we just wanted to hear the sound of our crackling voices for a little while longer. Nonetheless, something kept us going.

Sergeant Chris darted out of a sheet of rain. "What on earth are you four idiots doing out here yelling at the top of your lungs?!" he yelled.

Zhang responded, "Sargen, I need my water bottle. Very, very, very bad!"

We all laughed. Porter explained, "We were told by the squad leaders to do iron mikes. We weren't sure if they were watching us or not, so we just kept going."

John Chris put his head in his hands. He pointed toward where I assumed was the barracks. "Get back to the barracks, you goofy idiots."

With arms still locked, we limped on our floppy legs back to the barracks.

Back in my room, I laid in my sweat-soaked clothes digesting what just happened. It had felt so awesome to be part of a team, even if it was the losing, undisciplined team. I thought about the high I felt when yelling out the lunges, laughing when we were physically beat, and finishing the punishment together. I discovered that this was a different kind of satiating feeling. What just happened was better than anything a party, hangout, or any drug could provide. Here's what else I realized: I definitely could not have found that feeling on my own. "That was fun," I told Tommy.

He was asleep. Perhaps I was meant to be a team player, I thought to myself. Maybe getting with the program wouldn't be the worst thing, after all. If those before me had stuck with this program since 1884, then why couldn't I?

On a side note, the three people I was closest to in my first year were Tommy, Porter, and Zhang. It's interesting how hard times can produce some of the strongest of bonds.

The next morning, everything went wrong. I forgot to take out my trash, I forgot to wear black socks to formation, and my room almost failed my squad leader's morning inspection. As the flag glistened in the morning sun's rays and my platoon stood erect at attention, my hands rested on the wet, cold pavement of the guard path. I had had it with getting in trouble. Regardless of my actions, my squad succeeded *despite* me, my platoon succeeded *despite* me, and Bravo Company *managed just fine* without me. They didn't need me as much as I needed them. Squad Leader Din's late-night wisdom is what I needed along with Sergeant Chris' morning motivational speeches. I needed to feel the inclusion and the closeness that I felt on the guard path last night, the feeling of being part of, supported by, and an integral part of a team - this team. I was sick of the dirty looks I received when I was disrespectful or noncompliant. I needed to be part of the solution rather than the problem. I was one of the last problem cadets in my platoon, and I was getting more and more negative attention from Cadet Command.

"Do push-ups, Chauff!" Sergeant Chris ordered. Tommy, Zhang, and Porter snickered. "Something funny, guys? Want to join him?" Sergeant Chris yelled.

"No, Sargen." Zhang murmured.

"No, Sergeant!" Porter firmly said.

"No, Sarrnt!" Tommy yelled.

My usual repertoire of pushups was starting to get old. Outside of the classroom, I was failing. Just like in public school, I was once again the class clown, only this time, in the barracks - and it still wasn't working for me. Ten pushups. I remembered who I was and what I had done - that I should be able to take anything at this point. 20 pushups. 30 pushups. I had endured the constant barrage of criticism and slander from my Russian gymnastics coach for four years. 40 pushups. My mom had always been hard on me. 50 pushups.

Sergeant Chris ordered me to stand up, his voice falling on deaf ears. I was in a different place than the rest of the platoon. I was in an inner dimension - a dimension of personal breakthrough. Questions flooded my mind. Why did I even talk back to leadership? Why did I treat everything like it was a joke? Why didn't I just get with the program and join the club? Why was I so defiant at home and with my educators? Why? I thought I was above everyone and everything - the cadets, the leadership, my parents, and the program. 60 pushups and I was far past muscle failure. No more pride, I told myself. I had enough with the rebellious act and defiant speech. Where did it get me? It was time to buy into the program that has produced Fortune 500 CEOs, world leaders, and compassionate philanthropists.

Individuals can accomplish some things, but I learned

last night that teams could achieve just about anything. When I got to 64 pushups, my arms gave out, and my body fell to the ground.

Everyone in my platoon (against orders) was staring at me, mouths open; even the other platoon in the company, which had heard my labored breathing, was gawking at me. This time when I stood up, I stood a bit straighter. I put my shoulders back, my chest out, and my chin up. If everyone else was buying into the program, I could too. I kept my eyes locked onto the back of Tommy's head just in front of me. "It took 64 pushups," I thought and smiled.

Buy-in

At military school, students hold to a higher standard. Their rooms have to be kept clean, they must comply with cadet-leadership, and they are encouraged to give back to the unit (team) whenever and wherever necessary. New cadets are assigned to a squad (7-10 cadets), a platoon (20-30 cadets), a company (30-50 cadets), and the battalion (200-400 cadets). How do military schools get head-strong students like me to meet their standards? It's through discipline in the form of physical exercise, essays, and dissenting critique, but also in the way of positive incentives, such as cadet of the month, promotions, and recognizable accolades to be worn on the cadet uniform. A cadet's decorated uniform often reflects their hard work and achievements - the fruits of their labor. First, military school humbles you. Then, it builds you back up.

When I first arrived, the consequences I received for my behavior were not only essential but the best thing that could have happened to me. Later on, however, the incentives only enhanced my work ethic. I was motivated to reach for the stars.

When I bought into the program, I quit looking around and talking during formation. When it came time for room inspections, I kept still at attention while Din inspected my room.

At morning formation, I quit making jokes with Tommy and stood unwaveringly at attention. I quickly figured out there was a time and a place to goof around, and that time and place were not at formation. When I was asked by my leadership to take out the trash, I did so without an attitude.

It was at this point where real maturity set in. "Productive" became my middle name. Suddenly I was being recognized for my submission, and the accolades began to accrue generously. It was as though someone opened up the floodgates.

Positive peer pressure at military school can be compelling and useful. Those in the academy who are considered "popular" aren't those who wear the latest and greatest name brands to school. Nor are they recognized as the class clowns. They're certainly not considered part of the "party crowd," which only consists of a tiny group anyway. Let me define "popular" from a military school perspective. **The popular crowd consists of the hardest workers, those who "bought-in" to the program, and those who desire to lead and succeed. Anyone can do that.** When I bought into the program, I quickly, and naturally attracted, other like-minded peers. These peers evolved into my friends. This new group of like-minded friends challenged me to take push myself even more.

Friends in a System That Takes Us Higher

"You realize who's really there for you when you're at your worst." - Anonymous

And so my story continues.

Free time at the academy was suddenly replaced with physically and mentally challenging activities. My social media, unlimited browsing, mindless YouTubing, and overindulgent television watching became a thing of the past. I was now marching, executing obstacle courses, and going on squad/platoon/company runs. I've become accustomed to standing in formation, organizing my room, cleaning the dorm hallways, and much more. This new routine played a huge role in molding my character, for it became my new way of life at the academy.

In my first and second years, I spent around 40 minutes a day perfecting my military stance - the position of attention. At the time, it felt like a repetitive, dreary, painful waste of time. Eventually, however, it proved to be a considerable discipline booster. Standing at attention and doing other cumbersome activities made for bonding relationships with those in my squad, platoon, and company. These individuals are the ones who motivated me to push through. They were the ones who expected a change in me while I was at my worst. I began to look to them for help and encouragement, and so the transition from being just peers, to close friends, to brothers, began.

In the public school system, it felt like "each man for himself." At the forefront of my brain, I thought about who I could surround myself with and which parties to attend to climb that social ladder. I was also consumed with what I had to wear to "fit in" (one less distraction at a military school - all the cadets wear from the same *designer*), look the part, and how I could get ahead to improve *myself*. I was in my bubble, and those around me appeared to be no different. I attended public school up until the eighth grade. I've surveyed and can confidently share that though there may be pockets of unity, overall, this aspect is lacking - it is not the theme of the schools.

Nonetheless, I've continued to keep in touch with my old friends, now in high school. I've also solicited the opinions of several relatives who happen to be public school principals, and in doing so, I found their thoughts on this to confirm what I've observed all along. A comradery is taught and developed in military schools like no other. The phenomenon is so unique it's the antithesis of what most private or public schools have to offer.

I'm not here to point the finger at anyone or anything. I take full responsibility for who I once was and what I'm becoming. Nonetheless, the conventional educational system I was brought up in is one dimensional, flat, and lacking the character building blocks and life-changing experiences offered at a military academy. Also, I have found that unlimited use of social media and a constant obsession with smartphones is a distraction to comradery. Relationships tend to lack depth - for behind the high-fives, the barrage of snapchats, the latest gossip, and just hanging out, there appears to be a shallow connection. This obsession with social media has skewed any sense of reality with a focus on how many "likes" one can accumulate with their posts. Would perhaps limiting this technology in the schools encourage more face to face interaction? Has unmonitored use of smartphones stunted social interaction within the school system? I think so!

At St. John's, phones are prohibited during the first month of school, period. Also, during mess hall (meal times) and formation among other events, protocol prohibits the use of these devices to encourage in-person interaction. Phone privileges, like anything else, have to be earned, especially with incoming cadets. Perhaps there's wisdom behind limiting electronic devices. With the advancement of technology, face to face social interaction of any depth has taken a sharp decline. I experienced it first hand when coming home for holiday breaks. Reuniting with old friends was something I always looked forward to. However, I noticed the conversations were starting to decline in substance.

Two of my friends from my previous school have known each other since first grade. They are "best friends." I've seen them shoot hoops together, sleepover at each other's homes (at one point almost weekly), golf together, and bring dates to prom together. I have to wonder, however, if its a friendship of convenience or one that calls them both higher? Do they challenge each other to put their best foot forward? Where do their conversations lead? Deep into the statistics of fantasy baseball? Yes, they were in that fantasy baseball class together when I took that dreaded typing class. Both of these friends are very talented and bright indeed, but I've often wondered, "why are they holding back?"

At military school, cadets are taught to put others first. The cadets who buy into this think about how they can serve others to receive a higher rank or position; most do so to impact even more people. They shine their shoes, clean their tie bar, and make sure their uniforms are always perfect - they've figured out that their presentation represents who they are.

So, how did a system transform such a headstrong mule like me into someone that works hard, cares about others, and gives two cents? For anyone wondering, the system works like this. It's really quite elementary.

Hard Work + Helping Others + Meeting Standards => Rank Promotion = Gain Privileges + Increased Responsibility

"Meeting the Standard" means doing enough community service hours, following the rules, maintaining a good uniform, and keeping one's room clean.

A **"Rank Promotion"** allows a cadet to gain privileges. However, the cadet gains more responsibility as a result.

When a cadet doesn't **"Meet Standards**," they receive disciplinary correction as well as extra help from other cadets and faculty to in order to meet the standards.

While getting a promotion is an *individual* incentive, there are also *group* incentives - squad, platoon, and company level competitions. All of these contribute to the competitive aspect of the military school system - a system that truly brings out the best in youth.

The most important competition is the "Superior Company Competition." There are four to six companies of 30 - 50 cadets: Alpha, Bravo, Charlie, Delta, Echo, and Foxtrot. Throughout the year, the companies can work to earn Superior Company points by doing their best in graded school-wide in-

spections, events, and competitions. The following criteria also factor into the competition:
- Company average physical fitness scores
- Company marching scores (formation)
- Company average GPA
- Company average amount of community service hours

Highschoolers love to win. That's just how we're programmed. Thus, within each company, cadets help others improve their grades, become fit, and become better at marching. On the weekends, friends will even do community service together to help the company achieve this Superior Company status.

This system sets up a "no man left behind" mentality within the cadet companies. If someone is struggling, people help them In my second year here, whenever a student in my company had below a 2.0 GPA, four company members would go to his room on a nightly basis and ask if he needed help with anything. It was impressive, and I'd never seen anything like it before.

Essentially, the spirit behind this competitiveness is to bolster cadets and those around them to strive for their best. The competition creates a demanding yet rewarding environment which gives cadets a sense of accomplishment. When cadets improve themselves, they have thirty other members of a company that they can also help improve! It's a domino effect system that genuinely changes people's lives.

One of my closest friends at the academy is from China. I've known Geo for only four years, only one-third as long as I've known the friends in my previous school. Geo is my workout partner, my study buddy, and the friend I console with when I'm down. To study for a biology final, we spent an entire weekend in the confines of my small room, testing each other on hundreds of pages of information as if preparing for the debate of our life. We continued for hours back and forth until the volley of information was etched in our brains. That's friendship.

When Geo encountered an issue with a disrespectful cadet in his company, he came to my room and asked me for advice until a solution transpired. That's friendship. When I felt like giving up my leadership position, Geo carefully and methodically surveyed the situation and convinced me to persevere and stick with it. That's friendship. Every day, Geo and I would challenge each other to *do* and *be better*, productive people. We pushed each other to take ourselves higher. THAT is friendship. Shakespeare put it ever so beautifully.

> *"A friend is one that knows you as you are, understands where you have been, accepts who you have become, and still, gently allows you to grow."*

Geo enlisted in the Army to gain his citizenship. As I'm writing this, he is in basic training. He wants to attend the United States Military Academy at West Point. That's his current mountain. He's on his path, and he has motivated me to stay on mine. That's friendship.

If you can derive one thing from this, it's that friends are meant to keep you on your path. They are the support train, the fan bus, and sometimes even the road map to help redirect you from a dead end.

Lonely Hiking

When I bought into the system at military school, I was recognized and eventually put in a position of leadership. During my freshman year, I was in charge of a squad of six cadets. In my sophomore year, I was in charge of the school's color guard, a twenty-man team that raised and lowered the American flag each day.

This was a game-changer for me. With more responsibility came less free time and more work. I was now concerned about the welfare of those assigned to me. It was no longer just about my friends or me. With a new, military-style curve shaping my productivity sophomore year, I started to run into further problems. How was I going to get all of my work done?

I did what most newbie workaholics do - I stayed up later, sometimes most of the night. On my plate was a leadership position with constant planning and coordinating demands, a rigorous class schedule, and my first serious relationship. I found myself relying on energy drinks to keep up with my new-found responsibilities and relentless workload. Having bought into the system, I became organized, well-disciplined, and attentive to detail. My reputation within the corps of cadets and among faculty was looking up. However, to sustain my new-found status, I felt compelled to "live up" to what people thought of me. Such standards were too high for *me* to live up to.

Staying up late created an entirely new set of problems; now, I had night security breathing down my neck. Since day one on campus, I had fought with night security on going to bed. "Lights out, Chauff!" As if I didn't have enough to deal with, now this? I always greeted the night guards with sarcasm and rude remarks:

"My grades are fine. I should be able to go to bed when I want to."

"No, I'm not going to bed."

"This is stupid. Are you kidding me?"

"I'm staying up until I have all my homework done. Report me!"

One evening, before the typical 10:30 p.m. night guard check, I decided that I was not going to take any comments from the night guard. He came by while I was "in the zone," and I thought to myself, "I'm working hard. He can't tell me what to do. I'm above this."

Let me conclude with, while I may have won the battle; I most definitely did not win the war. The way I spoke and treated this night guard almost permanently cemented a weak relationship between us while putting a stain on my reputation at St. John's. Right when he keyed into my room, I stood up in my chair and yelled, "You have no business in my hallway. Please get away from my room!"

Oh, the audacity... of my behavior.

The night guard responded. "This is my job! Don't tell me where I can and cannot go." He left furious, only to leave me wondering what my consequences would be. It was too late to take it all back; somehow, in my pride, I was able to justify the banter.

The night guard took my comment and recorded it in the "duty log." People who had previously thought highly of me were now questioning my character. They were astounded with my interaction that reeked of arrogance. There was only one thing left I could do: face the music and shut up.

As I would realize months later from this situation, I become tunnel-minded in my studies. I had become a lonely hiker, one willing to alienate relationships and disregard authorities. While my productivity had doubled since my eighth-grade year, my family heard less and less from me. It got to the point where my mother would send me nonsensical memes like: "Call your mother she thinks you're dead" and "Ry you no call?" That last one got my attention as it had the stereotypical Asian man front and center with the words plastered on his forehead.

"Mom, really? My roommate is Asian! That's not PC!" I must admit, she cleverly got my attention, and I got the point. I also kept less in touch with old friends and additionally began isolating myself from my new friends like Tommy and Porter. I did this so I could focus on my studies. This mindset, however, proved to work against me.

A solid reputation, a girlfriend, and the work ethic needed to attain exceptional grades you would think is the recipe for happiness - wrong. This was not the case for me. My parent's only expectation for me was "to do my best." Regardless, I found myself pressured to perform; to fulfill the expectations of everyone around me. Waves of stress and pressure started to overtake me. Like clockwork each night, after tutoring peers, I would usually talk to my girlfriend for a few hours. Following this, my studying began. After having a few sips of an energy drink, I would start my homework at around 11:00 p.m. Usually, around 2:00 a.m., after being told by the night guard that I needed to go to sleep, I would move study session over to my bunk bed. I would cover my head, body, books, and computer with a dark black blanket in order to continue working on essential homework and rosters/schedules required for my leadership position. This work, many nights, would continue until around 6:30 a.m.: wakeup time. My weekends were no different. I would prep for the SAT, ACT, and other things I deemed necessary to help me "get ahead" in life.

Robot

"Chauff is literally a robot," I heard someone say as I was walking down to breakfast one morning.

Students would tell stories about me as they learned about my tendency to stay awake working until morning. Teachers and students alike believed that I never slept. I was prepared to sacrifice my health, my well-being, and free time to impress, satisfy, and live up to the expectations of everyone around me. I wasn't a robot; I was becoming a dysfunctional machine fueled by caffeine oil.

I was exactly what I termed earlier as a lonely hiker. I quickly learned that this was not the road to fulfillment and happiness. This was a trail up a mountain that would collapse into an abyss.

Earlier, I mentioned that the mountain to success includes deep valleys, thick jungles, and thin ice. In my current situation, I had abandoned my climbing team and was running full speed through the valleys, jungles, and across the thin ice without clothes, supplies, or food. In my mind, sleep and fuel were just holding me back from conquering my path.

The jungle quickly thickened, and I started to find myself feeling less and less "myself" as each week progressed. While most looked forward to Friday's approach to start the weekend festivities, I looked forward to Friday afternoons so I could crash. Subsequently, I would spend most of Saturday sick and in bed, and then cram on Sunday to get my work accomplished for the upcoming week. It became a miserable vicious cycle, a "rat race." I had to stop the insanity.

I came to realize I was nowhere near productive and was only making myself sick. After all, Albert Einstein once famously quoted, "Insanity is doing the same thing over and over again and expecting different results." So, I stopped my late night calls and my binge study sessions and submitted to the academy's bedtime schedule - going to bed between 10:00 and 10:30 p.m. and waking up between 6:00 and 6:30 a.m. I realized that this consistent sleep routine boosted my daily productivity by about threefold. For the second semester of my sophomore year, I was able to enjoy my evenings and complete homework during and immediately after class. While I used to fight from falling asleep during classes, I now found myself extremely alert with an ability to retain a vast amount of information, effortlessly.

If you could take one thing away from this book, having learned nothing else, I would like for it to be this: your body needs sleep.

A Sleep Schedule?

In seventh grade, one of my friends would always leave group hangouts to go home between 8:30 p.m. and 9:00 p.m. I always made fun of him for leaving so early, saying that he needed to stay on his "sleep schedule."

Regardless of whether my friend was actually on a sleep schedule or not, I had no reason to make fun of him. Scientific research asserts that adapting to a consistent sleep schedule is conducive to feeling energetic and "mindful" throughout the day. In fact, a full eight hours of sleep is necessary to ensure that you have enough energy to get through what is termed the "mid-day slump," a time of drowsiness between 1:00 and 3:00 p.m.

You're probably hesitant to give up your "late-night" cram sessions, phone calls, or anything you do that extends beyond 11:00 p.m. After all, you may be thinking, you've been "faring alright" so far. What would a headstrong teenager know about sleep?

Getting on a routine sleep schedule with at least seven hours of sleep will reap extreme benefits in your life. In my experience, I've found that going from sleep-deprived to seven to eight hours of sleep gave me more energy, which in turn improved my relationships with others. Why? Because now I was able to think beyond my feelings and onto the situations and feelings of others. I once thought that getting more sleep would leave me with less time to get things done. The opposite was true. Getting more sleep made me more productive and gave me more energy to accomplish what I needed to do. *That's* worth repeating:

Getting more sleep makes you more productive and gives you more power to get things done.

Sleep offers many other benefits cited by the U.S. Department of Health and Human Services:

- Getting sick less often
- Staying at a healthy weight
- Reduced stress
- Thinking more clearly
- Making better choices

Still not convinced? Let me tell you why sleep is *an essential* aspect of helping you succeed. Without it, there are little to no steps to the top, mountain climbing, or building of your platform. When you get on a sleep schedule, you will start to take charge of your day instead of just getting through it. You essentially become less emotionally driven and become more intentional. Let me explain what that means.

Think back to the last time you were exhausted. You were consumed with thoughts of when you'd be able to get to bed. You probably weren't thinking about how your actions that day could prepare you for the future or help you attain your goals. You definitely weren't wondering how you could help someone else get ahead - you were thinking about how to make it through the day.

Sleep notably makes up one-third of the average person's life. It is almost as essential as food for sustaining organs and healthy bodily functions. With sleep deprivation, according to *The Independent*, "Rats will die within two or three weeks - the same amount of time that it takes to die from starvation."

Several cycles span the average seven to ten-hour sleep period When these cycles are disrupted, studies have shown that individuals have less energy and feel more lethargic throughout the day. There's a phase of sleep called non-rapid eye movement (NREM). It makes up 80% of your sleep. During this time, slow delta waves essentially "charge" the brain and rewire its circuits, almost like an update on a cellular device. Neurons (cells) in the brain form memories, which help with declarative learning. One example of this would be memorizing terms for a test. You have heard that studying for an exam right before bed can increase your score. THAT is true. The other 20%

of sleep is composed of rapid eye movement (REM), or deep sleep. During deep sleep, long term changes occur throughout the brain, which allows for the transformation of short-term into long-term memories. Your brain is essentially downloading new data to compute from.

During REM sleep, hormones are released throughout the body, which repair and reproduce new cells, almost like construction workers. During sleep, your body updates - like apps on your phone.

Another study in the United Kingdom and Italy, which analyzed 1.3 million people and the deaths of over 100,000, further cited that higher comorbidity exists between lack of sleep and premature death. Furthermore, those who slept less than six hours a night were 12% more likely to die prematurely. Further analysis uncovers that those who reduced their sleep time from seven to five hours a night ended up having 1.7 times the risk of death. This is extremely startling. It must be challenging to be productive when you're six feet under.

Despite these statistics, sometimes work must still get done at night. However, like investing in public companies, one can and must invest in sleep at the right times. Kulreet Chaudhary, MD, emphasizes that the most powerful and regenerative sleep takes place between 10:00 p.m. and 2:00 a.m. During this time, the pineal gland secretes the most melatonin, or the body's signal to go to sleep. Around midnight, the average person's melatonin levels have hit their peak.

Around 10:00 p.m., many people report having a "second wind" of energy, which they claim helps them get started on their work for the night. Chaudhary claims that this second wind comes from the body beginning to repair its inner workings, the result of a rise of metabolic and mental activity, which is meant to restore the body during sleep.

Melatonin functions much like a clean-up crew - it's the janitors who clean the body. With around 37.2 trillion cells to clean, the janitors need all the time they can get to tackle this feat. Throughout the day, junk called "free radicals" accumulate within cells; as a result of stress, these large, harmful molecules can prevent efficient cell function. They are thought to be the cause of many short and long-term diseases such as cancer, diabetes, and dementia. To avoid a build-up of these potentially harmful molecules, the night "clean up crew" destroys and breaks them down while we sleep. Chaudhary's thorough research shows that staying awake past 10:00 p.m. causes this process to stagnate suddenly. Utilizing a bright phone right before bed also delays this process.

Regardless of the research, sometimes studying must go on. Late in my sophomore year, a student asked me about how he could cram a large project in just one night. Based on my own mistakes, this is what I was able to tell him.

"Stop your work and go to bed between 10:00 p.m. and 10:30 p.m. Ensure that you remain asleep for the most important four hours of sleep of the night: 10:00 p.m. to 2:00 a.m. Wake up, depending on how much work you need to get done, between 4:00 a.m. and 6:00 a.m. and work (with light caffeine) until you get the project done. Although you may be tempted to drink an inordinate amount of caffeine to stay up all night, this will adversely affect you in the weeks that follow. Investing in your sleep during the most important part of the night will afford you ample amounts of energy to complete the project in the morning and in the hours preceding your class."

This student finished the project with time and energy to spare. Like me, this cadet realized that the benefits of sleep far outweighed the costs of procrastination and cramming. I realized much later, every night guard that told me I needed to go to sleep, regardless of their motive, was right. I needed a healthy amount of sleep to sustain function and energy the following day.

SEVEN-NOBODY CARES ABOUT YOU, FORGET YOUR EGO

Nobody cares about you. Well, not really. People do care about you. However, they don't care about the things *you think* they care about. Let me tell you a story.

It's prom night. A freshman in high school, Adam has been stressing over his outfit for hours. He has had a crush on his prom date, Susan, since the sixth grade. Adam isn't sure if she likes him back, and doesn't want his appearance to ruin his chances. Little does he realize, of all his friends, he is wearing the coolest suit and tie. Unfortunately, the inevitable occurs. As Adam is looking into the mirror thirty minutes before his date is scheduled to pick him up, he notices two medium-sized pimples in the center of his forehead. Mortified, he calls his mother to the mirror and asks her for advice. He pleads, "I can't go to the dance like this!" She tells Adam that he looks fantastic and that he should look forward to having a good time at the dance with Susan.

Out of nervousness, Adam calls his date and tells her he is running late. Staring into the mirror fixated at his pimples, Adam's hands begin to sweat. Thinking of all the judgemental looks he'll receive at prom, Adam's "fight or flight" turns on.

Fearful for his social status, he decides to squeeze his pimples, a last-ditch effort to win; only they get worse. All Adam can focus on are his newfound imperfections and what Susan will think. As his insecurities get the best of him, Adam resorts to cover his face with his hands and sit on the couch and sulk.

Susan is extremely excited to attend prom with her date. However, she feels hugely self-conscious about her red, hourglass dress, which seems to be a size too small. After struggling to zip up the back, Susan finds that the dress puts pressure on her back and shoulders, making her feel noticeably uncomfortable. What makes her extremely uneasy is the thought that someone might notice her gown being too tight. The idea of any of her friends seeing that and making a comment frightens her - even worse, her date. Susan has had a crush on Adam since the fifth grade, but she isn't sure if he likes her in return. She thinks, "He is going to be turned off with me in this tight dress. What was I thinking?" Susan asks her mom about her dress, hoping to receive some reassurance.

Her mom replies, "Honey, you look beautiful."

Susan sarcastically replies, "Yeah, right."

Susan wonders about Adam's phone call. Why was he running late? Did he not like her after all? Did he not actually want to go with her to the dance? Why was he stalling for time?

Adam arrives to pick up Susan for the dance. Adam finishes wiping the tears off his face and meets her at the front porch, where the two, awkward freshman stare at each other petrified and riddled with insecurity. Adam wonders if Susan sees his pimples, and Susan wonders if Adam sees how small her dress is. All Adam sees is how beautiful Susan's new earrings and hourglass dress look, and all Susan sees is how handsome Adam looks with his new hairdo. Adam eases up and breaks the ice. Clearly blushing, he tells his date that she looks beautiful while they hug. Susan tells him that he looks exceptionally handsome and hugs him back.

In the car, Adam grabs Susan's hand, and they both forget about their appearance and sit together, in the moment. "Why were you late?" Susan asks.

"Don't worry about it. Long story," replies Adam.

Throughout the evening, both Adam and Susan regain their confidence. Nobody, including friends, parents, PTO members, or other students, comments about Adam's acne nor Susan's tight dress. The young couple enjoys their evening and even compliment other couples, who may have also felt insecure about their appearances. Susan even ends up becoming prom queen!

The moral of this story is simple. Nobody Cares. Everybody is self-conscious. Everybody cares so much about their own appearance, reputation, etc., that they could care less about yours. When Adam and Susan walked into prom that evening, they were amongst hundreds of their peers who were probably more insecure about their flaws than they were. Other teens may have been worrying about their haircuts, cologne, shoes, eyelash length; the list goes on. Most attendees were too fixated on their own insecurities and flaws even to notice Adam and Susans'.

In reality, everybody has their own insecurities, personality, and appearance flaws. Most individuals are incredibly self-conscious about these flaws. So much so, in fact, that they are too consumed to notice anyone else's.

At first, I was *extremely* embarrassed to wear my military uniform off-campus for fear that I was going to draw attention to myself. I didn't want to be thanked for service I never gave or asked about my "deployment" by a random person. But only after wearing my uniform off-campus a few times did I realize that *nobody cared*! Everyone in public was focused on their own day and saw me as just another, ordinary person walking around.

So many allow for their insecurities and self-consciousness to dictate the outcome of their daily lives, personalities, interactions, and fun. They allow simple flaws in their appearance to become "fight or flight" situations. For example, instead of enjoying a day with the family at the zoo, Steve Smith spends the day worried about how his new haircut makes him look. It makes him moody, unhappy, unsatisfied, and grumpy towards his brother and parents.

Some take their insecurities to a whole new level. They try to change their personality, appearance, hair color, gender, name, or any other thing about them just to get the attention or acceptance of other people. Here's what they don't realize. The praise and acceptance of other people will never be enough. A person may feel accepted after they change themselves for the approval of another; however, it leaves them feeling unfulfilled and empty. They eventually come to realize, "If I cannot be accepted for who I really am and if I need to keep changing myself in order to be accepted by this person and that person, then my true self is worthless."

Brendon Burchard, known as the world's leading high-performance coach, provides insight in his book, *High Performance Habits*. Burchard addresses this very issue:

> *"Most people aren't thinking about you at all," Burchard claims, "and even when you put yourself in front of them to make a request, and they say no, within minutes they're right back to not thinking about you. They're not sitting there judging you; they're too busy dealing with their own life."*

Do you really care what the drive-thru manager thinks about your haircut? Is the pimple on the side of your face really going to stop you from talking to someone? Is your boss' opinion about you going to prevent you from going above and beyond in the next project? Are the foul-balls of life really going to stop you from hitting a home run? Are your friends really "keeping you" from being more popular or adapting to a new fashion style?

Absolutely not.

Set the Trend

Consider the following quote from Steve Jobs, American co-founder of Apple Inc.

"The world is so much broader once you discover one simple fact. Everything around you that you call life was made up by people who were no smarter than you, and you can change it, you can influence it, you can build your own things that other people can use."

Think about the common trends that you see in magazines, television, or on the streets. These trends were made by people less intelligent or not much smarter than you. Think of the CEOs of today. At one point in their lives, they were once at your level. If you work hard, you can someday set trends, influence others, and also be termed "successful."

It's inevitable that some will interject negative comments about your deepest insecurities. They will criticize anything from a project you're tackling to a new hairstyle you decide to sport. I've received my fair share of disapproving looks or comments from people when I mentioned I was writing a book at fifteen. Some people dismissed me as crazy, and others told me I could never pull it off. Quite honestly, I was tempted to believe them.

I almost completely abandoned the idea of writing this book. What could I possibly know about writing a book, publishing a book, or any of that? I had an idea that was birthed through an unsettling interaction. I wanted to turn the situation around - to touch someone, anyone with my story. Stair by stair, I somehow, with God's blessing and the insight afforded me, found my way.

"So many people along the way, whatever it is you aspire to do, will tell you it can't be done. But all it takes is imagination. You dream. You plan. You reach." - Michael Phelps

When things get tough and we confront setbacks on the mountain, we tend to get caught up in the turmoil of our negative thoughts. We start to feel sorry for ourselves. When we begin caring about how we look to others, we forget who we are. We forget about our own goals and how we are going to achieve them. We stumble and then start to feel even worse about ourselves. We don't realize that having pity for our own situation is the equivalent of walking down the "success stairs" toward failure. That's worth repeating.

Having pity for our own situation is the equivalent of walking down the "success stairs" toward failure.

Everyone is *not* out to get you. In fact, most people don't even care about you, what you're doing, or your life "mission." The raw truth is this - people are too concerned about their own personal drama and insecurities to give much thought about yours.

"You probably wouldn't worry about what people think of you if you could know how seldom they do." - Olin Miller

Your worst enemy is you! It is *your* inner insecurities that hold you back from climbing those stairs, from moving toward success, and that falsely remind you that you're undeserving of success. You allow yourself to be barraged with this negative thinking and self-pity. You are falsely reminded of how unique your situation is and of the falsehood that success only comes to everyone else except for you. Turn off that thinking. It is toxic and self prophesying. I can assure you, someone else's situation is worse than yours. Get a grip on your thoughts as it is there where everything begins. You are not a failure!

> "Fear doesn't exist anywhere except in the mind." - Dale Carnegie

Imagine what you could do if you lived without *justified* fear - the type of fear that keeps you alive. This is *justified* fear - you have a six-foot grizzly bear suddenly 3 yards away from you. I'd say fear is warranted in this situation.

For so many years, I gave way to *unjustified* fear - fear of failure and others' perceptions of me. Here's why. I found that it was easier for me to make excuses for why I wasn't taking action instead of just taking action - it was easier for me to blame the 10% I couldn't control rather than own the 90% that I could change. This pattern of behavior is the number one reason why, in my opinion, mediocrity has become normal throughout America.

Taking Charge

A student once came to me seeking guidance. I asked him a set of questions, twice. When I asked him the questions a second time, he realized that he was blaming everyone except for himself for all of his problems. He finally "took charge" of his own situation.

The first set of questions and answers:

Why don't you have good grades? *Because I have bad teachers.*

Why don't you have friends? *Because people don't like me.*

Why aren't you athletic? *Because I don't have time in my day to exercise.*

Why do you disrespect your parents? *Because they are mean.*

Why are you not the best version of yourself? *Because of the reasons above.*

The realized set of questions and answers:

Why don't you have good grades? *Because I don't do my homework and study for tests.*

Why don't you have friends? *Because I play too many video games instead of socializing with others.*

Why aren't you athletic? *Because I don't make time for exercise.*

Why do you disrespect your parents? *Because I have an attitude problem.*

Why are you not the best version of yourself? *Because of me.*

    I wasted years of my life allowing my insecurities to dictate my existence. I was unhappy. For this reason, I plead with you to not let your insecurities get the best of you. Don't think that making excuses is going to get you any further! Excuses are just that - excuses - unjustified fear. Turn those negative voices off inside of you or the voices of others telling you, "you're not good enough." You have the control to choose what you listen to and pay attention to.

    Whether you want to attain wealth, grow spiritually, or start a nonprofit organization, you are the only person who dictates your outcome. It's not your friends patronizing you, or those who doubt your efforts, nor your school teachers, parents, or athletic coaches. Just you.

EIGHT-BE LIKE A CHILD

"My expectations were reduced to zero when I was 21. Everything since then has then been a bonus." - Stephen W. Hawking

Toward the middle of my sophomore year, I noticed that the relationship with my girlfriend was coming to an end. While I claimed I was "in love," what I really felt was just a "feeling" of love, or what Dr. Scott Peck terms to be cathexis in his book *The Road Less Traveled*. Mainly, I based my overall happiness on the state of the relationship with my girlfriend. I was attached. However, Peck's passage distinguishing cathexis and love had me squirming in my seat, evaluating my idea of love.

> *"When love exists, it does so with or without cathexis and with or without a loving feeling. It is easier - indeed, it is fun - to love with cathexis and the feeling of love. But it is impossible to love without cathexis and without loving feelings, and it is in the fulfillment of this possibility that genuine and transcendent love is distinguished from sim-*

ple cathexis.... True love is not a feeling by which we are overwhelmed. It is a committed, thoughtful decision... This person has made a commitment to be loving whether or not the loving feeling is present. If it is, so much the better; but if it isn't, the commitment to love, the will to love, still stands and is still exercised... In a constructive marriage, the partners must regularly, routinely and predictably, attend to each other and their relationship, no matter how they feel."

Love goes beyond high school prom. It goes deeper than late-night phone calls, gift-giving, and feelings. Love is a commitment; it is a choice.

Regardless of your beliefs, I believe that the best definition of love is found in the bible.

"Love is patient and kind. Love is not jealous or boastful or proud or rude. It does not demand its own way. It is not irritable, and it keeps no record of being wronged. It does not rejoice about injustice but rejoices whenever the truth wins out. Love never gives up, never loses faith, is always hopeful, and endures through every circumstance." - 1 Corinthians 13:4-8

If there's anything I learned from my three-month roller coaster ride, sophomore year, it's that a real relationship is never possible if you do not accept yourself but instead look for acceptance from the other person. I've already said it once, but it's worth mentioning again.

The praise and acceptance of other people will never be enough.

Many labor their entire lives, seeking the acceptance of others only to become increasingly miserable. Freshman year,

I thought that having a girlfriend would be the "be-all-end-all:" the grand-slam home-run solution to the complex problem of life. I knew my issue was unhappiness, but the underlying cause was a poor self-image. I didn't accept myself. I thought the only way I could gain self-approval was through having other people approve of me. However, even when I achieved that approval, it just seemed like it was never enough; it left a marked void in my heart.

A few months later, my path up the mountain caved in. My close friends sat me down and told me something no teenager ever wants to hear: "You and your girlfriend aren't right for each other - there's too much drama - enough already." Waves of negative emotions flooded my mind. I knew it was the truth, but I didn't want to accept it. After some consideration, however, I decided to end the relationship abruptly.

That was probably one of the lowest points ever. I didn't see a way out. I felt how many people think when they're in the cave - isolated, alone, a victim.

Being in the cave of a mountain can be worse than being on a dead-end path. In a cave, your senses are impaired. You can't see or think clearly, and you start losing it. Your decisions are based purely on survival, and you can't seem to climb your way out. I call these decisions "cave-man" decisions. Cavemen think based on their instincts - what many scientists refer to as the "Reptilian Brain" - the primitive portion of the brain responsible for keeping us alive. Cave dwellers only focus on essentials - finding food, water, shelter, and seeking warmth. They do whatever they can to get by. Cavemen do not live in the complexities of the 21st Century. They are unfamiliar with social media, college applications, and in most cases, social and moral standards - aspects of society which require the usage of the part of the brain right behind your forehead - the Prefrontal Cortex (PFC). The PFC is the planner, observer, and deep thinker of the mind. It is the portion of your brain that considers the short and long-term consequences of your decisions. When you make caveman decisions, you stop "thinking," in a sense, and you act on the urges of the "Reptilian Brain." **Those who can think clearly when they fall into a cave - an unexpected, undeserved, or random situation that life throws at them - are the most content and prosperous.**

When I fell into my cave, I sent an emotionally-ridden, "Reptilian Brain" filtered text to my girlfriend. Although I thought winning the battle by making her feel bad might help me exit my cave, I realized later that I had only dug myself deeper into this cave. In the depths, I figured something out the hard way:

Can two wrongs make a right? No. Instead, two mistakes make for two very discouraged people.

I was a broken soul. I felt terrible for myself, and I made even more "caveman" decisions like slandering my ex-girlfriend to anyone who would listen. I partook in immature acts of revenge (I'll spare you all the details) that only pushed me further into my cave. Looking back at my situation, the things I did were wrong. My senses were shut off - I had allowed my Reptilian Brain to take over. Every act I committed had woeful repercussions setting me further behind in my other relationships. I became the recipient of disapproving looks from friends and family of my ex. Even some of my fellow peers looked at me with foul glares. Regardless of how justified I felt or how warranted the circumstances, I was the loser.

I decided to make amends with those I hurt along the way. I managed to apologize to my parents, friends, and yes, even to my ex for the many ways I wronged them. It took me almost an entire year to reverse the consequences which my caveman decisions had caused, but it was well worth it.

Life Throws You in a Cave

The cave is an event in your life that you cannot control. It can be anything from being fired from a job to losing a family member. It can even be something as simple as having a bad day, being tired at a critical time, or just feeling demotivated. Life has a way of backing us all into a cave at some point. If you told me that you've never fallen into any type of cave along your journey, then congratulations - I encourage you to play the lottery since you're in the 0.00000001%! Being in the cave unequivocally stinks. Take note, however, that without a cave, which includes hardship, challenge, and inner tension, how would you be able to distinguish yourself from anyone else? What do successful people do when they enter a cave? They cope, seek out trusted friends and mentors, and fight through. Think about this. The more a person takes action, the more potential they have for encountering a setback, or getting out of "caves."

As I'm writing this, I'm thinking about the team competition I did yesterday in which I ran five miles - with a fever, low energy, and body aches. At the start of the meet, everything in me wanted to take the easy way out - to quit. However, I couldn't let the team down. When I pushed through, I didn't conquer physical barriers, but rather, mental obstacles. The truth is, in most cases, the cave is entirely psychological. Furthermore, the people who learn how to navigate through their caves are those who will genuinely grow, prosper, and remain happy in any situation. Had I quit, I would be missing out on the euphoric conquest I am now able to experience.

Merely recognizing what the cave is and accepting that you are in it will give you an edge for navigation. You will fight to find your path instead of just "accepting" the circumstances. Once you conquer a few caves, you'll see your mood improve, your self-image increase, and your journey moving in the right direction. You'll start to become a seasoned navigator, able to give guidance not only to yourself but to others as well.

The Hardest Lesson

"Let your enemies be disarmed by the gentleness of your manner, but at the same time, let them feel, the steadiness of your resentment." - Lord Chesterfield

    I'm challenging you to change your thinking and take it higher! I"m about to throw you a "pearl of wisdom."
    When someone wrongs you, do not wrong them back. Yes, this is a difficult teaching. In a sense, if you mistreat them in return, it means they have "won the war" over you, your character. If you wrong them back, you have compromised a part of you; you have become more like your aggressor. Second, a true leader has the maturity to forgive others. When others mistreat you and you choose not to stoop to their level, they eventually figure out that they have committed a wrong. Whether they admit it or not, they *will* feel uncomfortable in their inner core without you telling them or seeking revenge.
    If you have ever yelled at your parents, it may have felt good at the moment. The "glory" of "payback" may have given you energy and satisfaction. You may have ridden off on an imaginary chariot to your room as you basked in victory. Why did you feel justified? Did they make you clean your room, take out the trash, or encourage you to do homework? How audacious of them! While you may have felt temporary satisfaction, eventually remorse sets in for yelling at them or relaying a hurtful comment that once said can not be taken back.
    The problem with retaliation is that it goes hand in hand with sadness and guilt. This behavior, if repeated, defines who you are and depletes you of energy. On the other hand, doing the right thing fills people with a zest for life. You probably can't name a consistently happy person who habitually lies, cheats, steals, or commits crimes. Think about this. Has committing

something immoral ever made a drastic improvement in your life? No! In the same way, getting revenge on people will most certainly devour you and rob you of life.

> *"When you begin a journey of revenge, start by digging two graves: one for your enemy and one for yourself." - Jodi Picoult*

Remember what I said about controlling *your 90%* of the bargain? When you stick to your 90% of the deal, the other 10% tends to fall in your favor. Getting revenge on another person is like abandoning your 90% of the agreement and trying to control life's 10%. There is no controlling the other 10%. Thus, you will start losing control of yourself. I promise you that the loss of control will only rob you of your energy.

What Happened?

What happened to the innocent 4-year-old who enjoyed jumping in muddy puddles with friends? What happened to the toddler who could play at the park for hours without getting bored or exhausted? What happened to "the best breakfast in the whole wide world" being for me, honey-nut cheerios in milk? Expectations. Those things weren't good enough anymore. They no longer met the expectations. That's what happened.

Think back to when you were a child. Remember how the little things excited you, like your dad walking through the front door after a long day of work, or the smell of freshly baked bread permeating the entire house or the long-anticipated knocking on the door when the company finally arrived. Oh, the cheerful innocence and bliss of your childhood. Imagine if, in your current adolescent, adult, or senior life, you still felt the bright happiness of childhood. Imagine a world in which everyone felt the pure innocence of a child. Pause for a moment and think of how many world-wide issues would be obsolete.

If you ever attend a birthday party of a child under the age of seven, notice the unabashed running around, laughing, and smiling faces of the kids participating - they are uninhibited and full of energy. Games like tag, hide-and-go-seek, musical chairs, and Simon Says have a way of entertaining young minds for hours. For the most part, everyone participating in the games, win or lose, is laughing and enjoying the moment (I was too competitive to enjoy it at seven, but that's just me). For the most part, at such a young age, the children have very little drama, competition, or ulterior motives. They are happy to be taken care of, to be fed, and to be participants.

Think of all of the drama-filled situations you can avoid by just having the attitude of a child. Think of the last argument you got into with a fellow student, coworker, or family member. Remember, it takes two to fight. Maybe your dispute with them was based on how you perceived they *should* treat you. Perhaps it was over what they *should* have done.

Let go of your pride. How do you do that? You recount everything you have to be grateful for, and you tell yourself that so many others have it worse off than you. A helpful exercise would be to write down 10-20 of those grateful things on paper in black and white. Hang your list up in your room somewhere clearly visible to remind you multiple times a day why you have every reason to be happy.

Let me help you get started. According to the United Nations Development Programme, almost half of the world's population (three billion people) live on less than $2.50 a day. Most likely, if you own this book, then you probably make more money than that. Still don't feel grateful? Consider this. The United Nations Inter-agency Group for Child Mortality Estimation cites that 22,000 children die each day due to poverty. What makes you and me *not* deserve to be one of those children? In other words, what makes anyone of those children deserve their situation instead of us?

Can you think of anything else to be grateful for? What

about your family, the clothes on your back, and an abundance of food? What about your health? Perhaps a trip to the nearby cancer ward or a stroll through the impoverished housing projects might change your outlook on life? When St. John's sent me to volunteer at a nearby food pantry, my outlook changed. Close your eyes and imagine if those persons or items you cling to were one day gone; that to live a life without them would be devastating. Now understand what an opportunity you have to be something. Think of the opportunity you have to make an impact someday - to improve the situations of others using the resources that you now have.

If you take five minutes a day to consider the things you are thankful for, it could have a profound effect on you. Of those students whom I recommended to complete the "thankful exercise" daily, around 90% had an improved attitude over just one week. They started smiling more with a more positive disposition, thinking more about others, and focusing less on their problems.

When you're thankful for the things in your life, you begin to emit a glow of happiness that is real. Suddenly, when someone looks at you the wrong way, when someone over you reprimands you, when someone wrongs you, and even when you have an all-around lousy day, through this daily training of your mind, your thoughts now can shift to the good things in your life instead of how hard your situation is. You become happy again.

Stop having expectations. It goes along with being thankful for the things you do have. Without expectations, you will notice that you have more energy to do the activities *you want to do* in your day. Without expectations for how you think things *should* or *ought to* be, you aren't disappointed anymore. Instead, you are content with the things you *do* have.

Love the Least Person in the Room

One of my biggest mentors has been my dad. People naturally gravitate towards him. He invariably knows what to say, how to say it, and when to say it. Dad knows how to talk his way to the front of the line at the DMV. He knows how to make a joke arise from a painful situation. He knows how to talk the dentist into being more careful with my sensitive teeth.

From a young age, Dad reminded me that even more crucial than how I treated my superiors is how I managed those below me. It especially mattered how I treated the *least person in the room - the person with the least status*.

At family parties, I see my dad apply this principle flawlessly. He spends 80% of his time being loving to the elderly family members; this included my grandfather and several other 90+-year-old seniors. Usually, this group of seniors would sit in a corner at family parties, unable to freely communicate with others. For example, my grandfather has Parkinson's Disease, which causes involuntary tremors, problems with movement, and issues with working memory. Others who sat at his table had, in some cases, even worse ailments.

At one party, I noticed the entire family shift over to where my dad was sitting - with the elderly. Dad told me exactly why this happened.

"When people notice how well you are treating the 'least' people in the room," he told me, "they imagine in their minds that you will treat them much better. They think, 'If he is treating the least popular person in the room like this, imagine how he will treat me.'"

My dad also applies this to his health care business, resulting in outstanding patient care. I'll never forget shadowing him at work and observing him hold an older woman's hand before her surgery. It truly touched my heart the way he took the time to reassure her of how he was going to proceed. He whispered gently to her, "I'm going to administer anesthesia to you as if you were my older sister." He often took the time with each patient to explain precisely what he was about to do for them. As the anesthetic was about to be injected, he would softly speak in an almost paternal way. He would paint a vivid picture of everything they would feel: a tingling, burning sensation before going off into the deepest sleep they could imagine. "Before you know it, surgery will be over, and we'll be right here for you," he would say as his patients dozed off to sleep. I learned quickly that this was his way of consoling the patient before putting them to sleep.

People are always willing to do favors for my father. When he first started his business, three anesthesia providers (who had much more experience than dad) called him to say, "I'll quit my job and come work for you." Now, I understand why.

Putting It Into Practice

Dad once told me the start of his business began years back when he decided to apply his principles. Thus the beginning of a fifteen-year track record of being giving and loving was birthed. He practices this with both his patients and those he works with alike. He does this through his actions more than his words. From bringing in coffee for the on-call nurses to talking to patients after work, from offering to take people's night shifts to genuinely asking people about their day, he did everything without expecting anything in return. Almost every time my father would walk into the operating room, he tells me, he would put his hand on the monitor, smile, then say, "It's going to be a great day in room ___ today." The staff always looked at him with perplexity, but then the chuckles followed.

At military school, I learned that applying these teachings has to be **from the heart,** and it has to be done without expecting anything in return.

Zig Ziglar, a pioneer in the self-help industry and a New York Times bestselling author, holds the motto that "You can have everything in life you want if you will just help enough other people get what they want."

It's true. However, it takes genuine hard work. There is no manipulative route to impacting others to become successful in any way, shape, or form. I figured this out on my journey to create a volunteer-based peer-tutoring program in my junior year. There was no manipulating students to improve their grades or manipulating tutors to show up on time. That was something that hit me like a ton of bricks the first night of tutoring when only four out of the assigned 12 tutees showed up, and only five out of the designated 11 tutors showed up.

The next night, only two out of 12 tutees and three out of 13 tutors showed up. I went back to my room feeling discouraged and hopeless. Then the negative thoughts trailed. Thoughts of "you're not good enough" and "nobody will ever listen to you" flooded my head. I was tempted to abandon my idea and move on. For about ten minutes, maybe longer, I looked into my smudged mirror. I started asking myself questions like: *Who was I doing this for? Was it for the cadets or me?* I recognized that though I had a passion for this program, it was a moment of truth for me to realize and admit that the program was something I was doing more for me than for the struggling students. It was at that point I decided to change that. I was going to do it 100% for those students who wanted the help. I focused less on developing a program and more on helping those students, and I stopped expecting. I stopped anticipating that my tutors would show up on time, and I stopped expecting for the tutees to show up on time. I even lowered my expectations for students to improve.

What I did expect was to keep my attitude in check. I had to stay out of negative mode, maintain genuine motives and a clear vision for each tutee. So I focused on the little things. I would bring coffee to students in the tutoring center who seemed lethargic, help struggling students organize their rooms, and write tutors and tutees encouraging notes of appreciation. These notes proved to be encouraging for both; however, they served mainly as a reminder to me - to do things from the heart.

What did I know about running a tutoring program? I can't manage Google Sheets, I have a caffeine addiction, and I have an awful memory. At the time, however, none of those things mattered. I was determined to be the most positive man on the face of the earth - every day, I would tell my tutors and tutees that it was going to be a "great day at St. John's Northwestern Military Academy." Sure, sometimes it came through a bit sarcastic, but it worked. People started to believe it, and the days eventually became great. Students began showing up. Tutors were prepared, on time, *and* I found a special team to help me develop the program's logistics.

The impact this program had on the cadets has forever changed me. At one point, while contemplating quitting, I remember one student in particular who approached me told me that my tutoring program had prevented his suicide and changed his life. Another student shared with me that while I tutored him, he went from all D's and F's to a 3.5 GPA, followed by an acceptance to Augustana College. Shortly after that, the Dean of students shared that the peer tutoring program had a profound impact on increasing the school-wide GPA.

When students saw that I had authentic motives and that I enjoyed running the tutoring program, they bought in as well. The rest is history.

I focused on the students, and it improved the program. I focused on the steps, and it brought the program to new heights. It certainly wasn't all me. Many tutors were beyond helpful. One night, six tutors stayed up until 11:00 p.m. to finish tutoring rosters. Many served in the tutoring program as a favor to me - the kindness displayed to them was freely returned, and for that, I am grateful.

Your Turn

The next time you go to a party or social gathering of any kind, give it a try. Instead of going straight to your friends, spend

your first 15 minutes at the party with the "least popular" person at the party. As trivial as it may seem, it will accomplish the following things.
- Make you feel good
- Attract attention from everyone around
- Encourage whoever you are talking to

It's not about you, but rather, those around you. Remember that. Practice being kind to everyone. Treat others the same way you would treat your best friend or how you would like to be treated - with respect, kindness, and appreciation. Make sure that you are genuinely kind - most people can spot a phony, miles away. We've all heard the phrase, "What goes around comes around." You'll quickly see the "come around," some way or another. Do not expect, and good things will come back around. However, do not be surprised when adversity bestows you; when you have no expectations, you will also be prepared to handle whatever comes your way, even the bad.

Gossip

Watch any TV show that revolves around a scandal for its "hook." Examples include *Elite* and *Gossip Girl*. As you watch these shows, you may feel enthralled with certain characters who appear to have an "awesome life" being popular and talking down about less attractive people. However, as the episodes continue on, you will notice that these characters are overall unhappy. Interesting how even Hollywood gets that concept.

Think back to the last few days. Have you slandered anyone? The dictionary defines it as such:

> *"Make false and damaging statements about (someone).:*
> *'they were accused of slandering the head of state.'*

Did you misrepresent someone recently? If yes, then your realization of this lies within your conscience.

As almost everyone feels insecure about themselves, they seek to replace that feeling in several ways. Teenagers (though not immune to adults) boost their confidence by talking behind others' backs. By spreading gossip and talking about others' flaws and misdoings, the focus is no longer on them and what their shortcomings may be. So an attempt to divert the attention on someone else's weakness somehow becomes the solution for this individual's uneasy feelings. This immature behavior from the insecure teen is an attempt to feel better about themselves. In reality, it's an illusion, a deflection that only leaves the offender feeling worse. I know as I've experienced it many times. I'm not sure which feels worse, being the recipient of gossip or the instigator.

Gossiping about others is like trying to fill a vortex in your heart - it will never be full.

For adults, teenagers, or whatever stage in life you are in, it's crucial to avoid being this type of person. Instead, try to only talk positively about your friends, and more significantly, your enemies. Notably, **talking favorably about your enemies makes you look good**. That's worth repeating.

Talking positively about your enemies makes you look good.

Now hear this: **Treating your adversaries as if they never wronged you makes you look the best.**

As I said, it was a bad breakup in January of my sophomore year. After it happened, people approached me to get the "scoop." For the first several weeks, I found no issue with divulging the minutiae of the breakup. Of course, it was presented in a fashion of "victimization" - yes, I said that I was the *victim*.

After several weeks, I noticed that people had started to treat me differently - to view me cynically. Although they had curiously asked me to share the story, I noticed that they trusted me less. It took me back to something Dad said to me when all of this transpired. He said, "Son, careful what you say about your ex... whoever you tell is probably thinking, 'If Skyler is going to talk badly about this girl he once was smitten by, then maybe one day he'll talk badly about me.'"

My friends approached me with ambivalence; I could sense their distrust. It came out in subtle ways. They seemed distant. It wasn't with words that I could feel the separation, it was more from the lack of words said. Anytime a rumor spread about her, it was always traced back to me, regardless of whether or not I was the source. At that point, it didn't matter - it all came back to me.

What did I learn? When slandering someone, it doesn't matter if the information you are putting out there is accurate or not. In reality, you are talking bad about another person to:

A. Make them look bad, B. Have power over them, C. Ruin their reputation, and D. Momentarily make yourself look good.

Go ahead. Call your friends and gossip about the latest situation. At the end of the day, it is *you* that will reek of distrust. Even listening to gossip about others could blemish your reputation - I've seen it time and time again. Whether instigating or participating, the outcome is always damaging. Don't believe me? Think of all of your peers, friends, and acquaintances. Which of these people or person do you retort to whenever you want to hear about the latest gossip? Now imagine, since this individual is so inclined to divulge other people's secrets and misdoings, how likely are you to share your deepest feelings and insecurities with them? Most likely not.

Chances are, what you tell another person, in confidence, will most likely be shared with their best friend "in confidence." This "best friend" will most likely also tell another friend "in confidence." If your information is "juicy" enough, the next thing you know, many people will find out about it "in confidence."

NINE—WHERE "SELF" ENDS UP

Sophomore year was a lonely period for me. I spent most of my time working on my own self-improvement. Everything I did was tailored toward the notion of "self." Completing homework to get good grades for *me*. Practicing piano to soothe *me*. ACT studying to improve *my* score for *myself*. Volunteering in the community to earn community service hours to make *me* look good. Basking in shallow, meaningless conversations with friends on the weekends to have fun and give *me* a break.

Each week, I stood in Chapel, turned off all my thoughts, and recited the pamphlet that I had memorized. "Lord God, heavenly Father, we have sinned against you," I mumbled. A common rote practice always on Tuesdays, Thursdays, and Sundays during mandatory Chapel. Then I would walk back to my room, cursing and joking with friends.

Each morning, I would wake up and look at my overflowing desk, strewn with half-filled notebooks, scribbled on post-its, and half-read books. Then I would look into the mirror and ask, "What am I missing here?"

My life should feel whole, I thought to myself. At the time, I had friends, a girlfriend, and a decent reputation. I had goals, I worked hard, and I was self-motivated.

So, what's the problem? It felt like I had reached into a drawer and taken out every key except the one I needed for fulfillment.

I must have been missing the accolades posted on my door - goals for my future, I thought. Did I need more awards on my school uniform? Maybe I was missing out on a new group of friends. Perhaps I was missing that perfect score on the ACT.

I reached my hand deeper into the drawer and searched for the key. Then I searched for it in several other drawers. I bad-mouthed people, sought revenge on my enemies, and broke off relationships,which I didn't deem vital to my success and grabbed for the things that I believed would make me happy. I kicked my best friend off of the Color Guard (flag presentation team) because he wasn't "disciplined enough." I removed another close friend from this same group for showing up five minutes late to practice. It wasn't uncommon to confine myself in my room to study. I even stopped looking adults in the eye when they talked to me. I began to disregard people who, according to the self-help books on my shelf, weren't classified as "high achievers."

In times of stress, I would turn to unhealthy habits. If I was anxious about a test, I would bite my nails down to the bone. If I was stressed out about my relationship with my girlfriend, it would paralyze me in all other aspects of my life. If I was tired at the end of the night, I relied on food to soothe my nerves. I became moody and inconsistent.

The chase for some feeling continued. More and more negativity entered my life.

This hole eventually swallowed me. As I broke off relationships that I deemed "went against my success," I fell deeper and deeper into a lonely state. While my friends attempted to reach out to me time and time again, I was too busy chasing a score that my ACT textbook could hopefully provide. When I broke up with my girlfriend, I sought revenge, and then felt even more lonely. I was looking for *the* key in all of the wrong drawers.

The Constant

I have found in my life and in observing the lives of others at military school, a constant which spans all cultures, religions, and continents. It's a promise that guarantees that those who commit to doing wrong will become unhappy, and those who are committed to doing what's right will obtain happiness. Whether you believe in Karma or destiny, Christianity or Buddhism, probability or horoscope, evolution or creationism, there is an invisible force that rewards goodness and punishes evil. This invisible force has been acknowledged for thousands of years by everyone from philosophers to academicians.

> *"Every action has an equal and opposite reaction. This is the law of the universe, and it spares none. Wrong done and injustice inflicted is paid back in the same coin. No one has escaped the justice of the universe. It is only a matter of time." - Anil Sinha*

Eventually, everyone gets what they deserve. I have seen this played out again and again in military school. Selfish leaders lose the respect of their platoon; disrespectful platoon members fail in a leadership position once they attain it. Students who focus solely on their own well being tend to exude discontentment and sorrow. Cheaters and thieves eventually get caught, and liars ultimately get lied to. Take a close look at the consequences of people's actions, and it will become clear that one's fate unquestionably reflects the decisions they have made. Leonardo Da Vinci suggests this when he says, *"Realize that everything connects to everything else."*

It isn't until poor decisions pave for them an ill-fated side trail that many people start to make the association between poor choices, actions, deeds, and their current situation.

"Still others commit all sorts of evil deeds, claiming karma doesn't exist. They erroneously maintain that since everything is empty, committing evil isn't wrong. Such persons fall into a hell of endless darkness with no hope of release. Those who are wise hold no such conception." - Bodhidharma

Many fail to take charge of their lives. They remain stagnant. They cling to the side of the mountain, oblivious to their actions and decisions, until an avalanche hits.

Life hikers also invest in the wrong types of gear. They obsess over having a strong body, the most fashionable clothes, and the latest technology. They overlook the apparatus which will get them the furthest - their core values, their "why" list, and determination. As a result, they put down on other hikers, get caught up in gossip, and become crippled by life's avalanches.

"Whatever you give in life, it gives you back. Do not hate anybody. The hatred which comes out from you will someday come back to you. Love others. And love will come back to you." - Author Unknown

Shortly after breaking up with my girlfriend, I hit rock-bottom. I lost my enthusiasm to study, I lost my zeal in general, and I felt like giving up. I had entered the deepest part of my cave.

Looking back, I'm grateful I endured what I did. I'm glad I realized that looking solely out for my well-being and always trying to please myself is what eventually made me the *most* unhappy! I was hyper-focused on paving my trail to **success** *and happiness* that I ended up achieving just the opposite - unhappiness. My accomplishments became so meaningless that I always looked for **more.**

Arrived at the Cupboard

Quick author's note. I'm a nobody. I am not a world-renowned researcher. I am not an academic prodigy. I am merely a transformed young adult who wants to present information to you from a different perspective - my perspective. I hope to inspire you to either take action or investigate further. It just so happens that events in my life have triggered my search that led me to this new way of thinking.

It was an early, cold, dark, January morning. I did what I knew to do - I called my mom and whined and complained about my breakup. Her clear voice always resonated with me - she was the voice of reason. I was unsettled, not knowing what to expect, but I anxiously awaited for some reinforcement. My head was pounding from the turmoil I had created just days earlier. Mom didn't believe that anyone should feel sorry for themselves. For one hour, she didn't say a word as I grumbled, complained, and made excuses about why my situation was going south. When I finished, she asked if I had anything else to add, and I hastily replied, "no, I don't believe so." She then texted a bible verse to my phone.

> *"Do all things without grumbling or complaining; so that you will prove yourselves to be blameless and innocent, children of God above reproach ..."* Philippians 2:14-15

What? What was that supposed to mean? After some time, my mother began to speak. She told me to think about Jay, my brother, who was adopted at only three years old from Russia. I thought of the orphanage, with its leaky roof, filled with children of various ages. I can recall snack time as the kids were doled out slices of apple that had turned brown - the children did not know any different. The ratio of child to adult was 50, 60, maybe 70 to one, and it had me mesmerized. I remembered the emaciated stray cats that roamed the streets - some seeking food, some looking for an owner, some just longing for a good back-rub. I thought back to when I first laid eyes on Jay. His blondest of blond hair, blue eyes, and noticeably red chubby cheeks stood out, along with his timid stance. As he stepped through the creaky, wooden doors of the orphanage in Orenburg, Russia, he winced his eyes as if he had never seen the light of day. Although he didn't know who I was, he immediately ran up to me and hugged me. His bubbly smile welcomed love. By the time we landed on American soil, Jay had already learned three new words: "friend," "car," and "cereal."

I started complaining again. Mom cut me off. She continued by telling me about the ten-hour plane ride back from Russia - Jay's first time on a plane. She went on to share about the conditions surrounding Jay's situation. She also reminded me of the transition Jay had to face coming from a familiar surrounding, leaving all he knew and was attached to, and entering unknown territory. For months Jay communicated via sign language, slowly adding to his limited English repertoire. I knew she was trying to make a point, and so she continued.

Several months after Jay joined our family, while he was lying in bed next to mom, Jay said, "I thank God for my family." That phrase was forever etched in my brain.

What's interesting is that my family was supposed to adopt Jay's cousin, Ruslan. Well, it didn't work out. We still have no idea why we were given Jay. At the last hour, we were abruptly told that Ruslan was no longer available.

I've always been puzzled as to why Jay said what he said to my mom. He was only three years old and barely knew English.

When I got off the phone with mom, I was flooded with a plethora of questions. How did Jay know who God was when they had never talked about God in his orphanage? Was God real? If God was present, did he play a role in our lives, or did he just spin the world into existence? Then I started digging - researching, reading, studying. If there was an involved creator of the universe, I did not want to be left out.

I started my search by reading *A Case for a Creator* by Lee Strobel. It was a quick read, just enough to keep my attention. Lee Strobel is an ex-atheist turned Christian who also came into the realization that God existed after much research. For someone with a law degree from Yale, digging deeper was no simple task. I want to address two aspects of his book - Strobel's debunking of Darwinism and his analysis of the probability that the universe just "popped" into existence. Strobel states the following in his book:

> *"Looking at the doctrine of Darwinism, which undergirded my atheism for so many years, it didn't take me long to conclude that it was simply too far-fetched to be credible. I realized that if I were to embrace Darwinism and its underlying premise of naturalism, I would have to believe that: 1. Nothing produces everything 2. Non-life produces life 3. Randomness produces fine-tuning 4. Chaos produces information 5. Unconsciousness produces consciousness 6. Non-reason produces reason.... The central pillars of evolutionary theory quickly rotted away when exposed to scrutiny."*

Later, he goes on to explain one aspect of exactly how "lucky" we are to be alive.

> *"One of the most striking discoveries of modern science has been that the laws and constants of physics unexpectedly conspire in an extraordinary way to make the universe habitable for life. For instance, said physicist-philosopher Robin Collins, gravity is fine-tuned to one part in a hundred million billion billion billion billion."*

> *"The cosmological constant, which represents the energy*

density of space, is as precise as throwing a dart from space and hitting a bulls-eye just a trillionth of a trillionth of an inch in diameter of Earth."

These are just two aspects of our "luck." Hitting the dart from space does not include the chance of having a moon, having the right-size planet, and having the needed chemistry to sustain life.

What does that mean for Atheists and non-believers alike? Atheists have faith that the dart, without the guidance of any kind, just magically hit the bullseye, allowing for perfect circumstances for life to simply spring into existence. Let me repeat it - that is their *faith*. What has a higher probability - the universe conforming to an astronomically low probability or the universe being created by a god? That is for you to answer. Perhaps God spun the world into existence, I thought. Does he, however, play a role in our lives? Is he interactive on a day to day basis? How does one have a "relationship" with him? My search continued.

In Jay's one-room orphanage, there was no talk of God - Jay's limited vocabulary only consisted of a handful of Russian words (God was not one of them). How could Jay know who God was? Did God speak through him? Was he repeating what he had heard? To this day, I still don't know for sure, but I have a theory. The incident provoked deep thought, and what I discovered has forever changed my life.

Why do certain things "feel" wrong and other things "feel" right? Where does guilt come from? What does it mean to grow spiritually?

Through reading, researching, and talking to Christians, I learned that spiritual growth is a mere growth of the subconscious through conscious effort. It's a rewiring of the way we think. When we make a conscious effort to push away those negative thoughts and replace them with positive ones, eventually, we create a new pattern - a positive one. Unfortunately, it's not that easy. Several renowned authors have confirmed such a theory, referring to a "guiding spirit" that helps us along the way to changing ourselves for the better - something that we cannot do on our own.

In *The Road Less Traveled,* M. Scott Peck, M.D., affirms that God, grace, love, and mercy take root in the subconscious.

> *"With the learned capacity to recognize the gifts of grace, we will find that our journey is guided by the invisible hand and unimaginable wisdom of God with infinitely greater accuracy than that of which our unaided conscious will is capable."*

Even back in 420 B.C.E, Greek Philosopher Plato talks of the blamelessness and the guiding spirit of a God.

> *"When speaking of divine perfection, we signify that God is true and loving, the author of order, not disorder, of good, not evil. We signify that he is justice, that he is the truth, that God is love, that he is order, that he is the very progress of."*

When we look back at our lives, we come to realize that everything fits together like a puzzle. Plato's reference to God as "order" and "the very progress of" signifies that God may be within everyone. Whether we believe in him or not, he takes root within our lives from birth. Could God be the master of the puzzle?

We may be able to recognize that at specific points of our lives, even the slightest of changes would have put us on a completely different trajectory. For example, if we hadn't met a particular person, if we had not pursued a specific hobby, or if we had not acted a certain way to someone.

Whatever your situation, goals, failures, or life story,

think outside of it for a second. The bible says that God created every hair on your head.

> *"Indeed, the very hairs of your head are all numbered. Don't be afraid; you are worth more than many sparrows." - Luke 12:7*

He created every cell in your body. He engineered every water molecule, every grain of sand, and every living cell on the face of the earth. God didn't stop there. He created color (you realize he could have just left everything in black and white), smell, and sound for our enjoyment. He invented the northern lights, the beautiful moon, and the dazzling stars in the sky for us to enjoy.

This amazing God continues to grow trees, spin the earth, and even micromanage the relaying of chemical signals in the most complex machine in the world - the brain.

> *"Therefore I tell you, do not worry about your life, what you will eat or drink; or about your body, what you will wear. Is not life more important than food, and the body more important than clothes? Look at the birds of the air: They do not sow or reap or gather into barns - and yet your heavenly Father feeds them. Are you not much more valuable than they? Who of you by worrying can add a single hour to his life?" Matthew 6:25 - 27.*

God created the world. He continues to sustain the 37.2 Trillion Cells in your body. Did God skip over you, or me, or other people? Are you the exception to the rule? No! Even though circumstances become hard at times, it is all for a reason.

"For I know the plans I have for you, declares the LORD,

plans to prosper you and not to harm you, plans to give you hope and future." -Jeremiah 29:11

God wants to lavish you and me with an abundance of gifts! Do our poor choices, however, block him from doing this very thing that he so desperately wants for us? He won't make us do what he wants - it's not in his nature to; furthermore, we aren't robots that he programs to "do this and do that." God is purposeful, just like the universe was created purposefully. There are just too many "coincidences" to believe that everything is only a product of chance.

I'm not a theologian; I'm just a kid who decided to one day do his research and use common sense. If your entire life, thus far, has been a string of failures, suffering, sadness, and depression, I encourage you to turn things around! When you *do* it, you'll have the energy to help others do the same!

When I figured out that God was indeed real, I learned not to stress out as much in situations; especially under the direction of Gwen Lara, national best-selling author and founder of Weigh Down, a faith-based pioneer weight loss program. In her eight books, she explains how to have a relationship with God on an intimately personal level. Throughout her books are endless testimonials of people who have turned their lives around by putting bible-based principles into practice. Such individuals have lost 10, 50, 100+ pounds in addition to overcoming addictions to drugs, porn, or cigarettes. Others have overcome anxiety and depression. Through Gwen Lara's direction, I saw my life change. I would recommend reading any of her books, which provide life-changing, practical, everyday insight on how to resurrect change in your life.

"The bible says to pray without ceasing. Therefore, every hour is spent talking to him, asking him to help with clothes, work, difficult situations, asking him to rule my

day, asking him to find my keys, thanking him for something that just happened, coming to him for comfort from pain in the heart, and looking to him for his attention or approval and leading any way I can get it." - Gwen Shamblin-Lara

I used to stress out about many things. Now, when I'm feeling pressured, stressed, or anxious, I think, "Well, if God had a plan to create the universe, if God had a plan for the birds, and if God even went so far as to number all of the hairs on my head, then surely he can help me get through this situation." So I pray. I tell God exactly how I'm feeling and exactly what I want. When I do what is right, God works things out for me. However, when I act up, commit wrongful acts, or do what is "wrong in his sight," God does not honor that - nor answer my prayers. At first, the problem was that I wanted the answered prayers and a relationship with him on my terms; however, that was not what *He* wanted.

"If you abide in me, and my words abide in you, ask whatever you wish, and it will be done for you." Jn 15:7

Mrs. Lara emphasizes that we are all God's kids. What father would not want to bless his kids? God wants to bless you! Don't you believe that the creator of the world can do a better job at getting you what you desire than you can on your own?

Motivation

One of the things that sparks my interest is motivation. Where does it come from? Why, despite your genetic commonalities with your parents and siblings, do you have different motivations than they do? How is it that you can have one child in a family driven to get up at 5:00 a.m., fearful that there aren't enough hours in the day to accomplish all that needs to be done, and another child who has no problem sleeping in until 11:00 a.m. with not a care in the world, but just happy to see what the day will bring? Why do some people want to become attorneys while others want to become mathematicians? Quite honestly, when I looked in the direction of cognitive neuroscience, I found more unanswered questions than I had answers.

Bear with me. The brain is composed of cells called neurons. In order to form thoughts, memories, and experiences, neurons send each other chemicals called neurotransmitters, which are responsible for conveying "feelings."

To effectively influence another neuron, a neurotransmitter must "fit" into the receptors of another neuron.

Dopamine is a neurotransmitter in the brain. Dopamine spikes during moments of motivation and pleasure. Hence the name: "Dope." If the dopamine neurotransmitter is unable to fit into the receptor of another neuron, then that neuron will not be activated. Let's use an example: opera. When you see and hear opera, the brain's pathways which "see" and "hear" will relay these senses to the part that perceives images and sounds. Then, a chemical reaction will occur. For some, this chemical reaction causes dopamine to be produced in the rest of the brain, i.e., those who enjoy opera. For others, just the opposite occurs, and opera does not activate "pleasure" in these individuals (I get that). Why do some people like to watch opera and some don't? Is the answer found in genetics?

Some might say the proverbial, "It is in your genes." I don't buy it.

Every single cell in your body has a nucleus. This nucleus, the control center of the cell, contains the complete set of genetic instructions for how the cell grows, develops, and communicates with other cells. These genetic instructions, or DNA, essentially code for the creation of proteins. Proteins are the "muscle" and "function" of the cell, typically facilitating all actions throughout the cell.

In the neuron, proteins shape the receptors and are responsible for the making of neurotransmitters. Proteins are shaped by the DNA and genes of a cell. As we've learned, the receptors and neurotransmitters are responsible for the transference of information, feelings, and overall experience in the brain. However, a hole in this logic remains.

How can the genetic coding for proteins determine if an individual likes opera? The answer: it is too complex to understand. There is no simple answer to why one person likes opera and another doesn't. Analyzing the cognitive neuroscience left me with no other explanation other than a higher force is at play.

The subconscious is more complicated in more ways than can be perceived; therefore, I believe that God, to an extent, has birthed motivation and feelings in us. Scott Peck describes the value of trying to understand the daunting subconscious portion of the mind:

"If you work long enough and hard enough to understand yourself, you will come to discover that this vast part of your mind, of which you now have little awareness, contains riches beyond your imagination."

Your Sixth Sense

"Watch your thoughts, they lead to attitudes. Watch your attitudes, they lead to words. Watch your words, they lead to actions. Watch your actions, they lead to habits. Watch your habits, they form your character. Watch your character, it determines your destiny. - Unknown

The principles ahead are the tools to get you up to the peak - your roadmap to the top. A lifestyle that centers around such principles comes with more pleasure than the best drug, food, or exercise program. Side effects of this include but are not limited to often smiling, overflowing laughter, light-heartedness, peace, overwhelming confidence, an abundance of friends, prosperity, etc. Please apply responsibly.

Think about it - you have always had an innate sense of right from wrong. The first time you stole, you felt terrible afterward. When you lied to your parents for the first time, you felt an uneasiness, call it guilt. When you spoke maliciously about a friend, you later felt lousy. When you first cheated on a test, it left a bitter aftertaste in your mouth, otherwise known as guilt.

For some reason, guilt is the sixth sense which is programmed within us. I wouldn't be able to explain the neuroanatomical pathways responsible for guilt, but we can simply agree that guilt doesn't feel right. It makes us rethink our actions, have regrets, and feel drained of our energy.

In the short-term, guilt robs us of time and energy. A study cited by an *Independent Minds* article found that the average British person spends six hours and 36 minutes every week feeling guilty. That's roughly 14 days each year, 70 days in five years, and 140 days in a decade wasted on self-pity. That time that could be spent helping others, improving themselves, or just enjoying the amenities that life has to offer. Imagine if, right before the new year, time paused for 14 days, and you were able to get ahead during that time. Those 14 days could be the difference between you getting or not getting a future job, attaining or not attaining an offer from a dream client, or maybe even you learning or not learning a new language, trade, or profession.

Unabating guilt decreases our sense of worth, our self-image, and it deprives us of vigor. It robs us of positivity, makes us less productive, and puts us in a constant mental cave. Guy Winch, Ph.D., of *Psychology Today* gives a near-perfect description of the feeling of guilt.

> *"Unresolved guilt is like having a snooze alarm in your head that won't shut off. If you had a snooze alarm that never shut off, it would be hard to concentrate, as your attention would be constantly hogged by bursts of guilty feelings."*

Guilt from persistent wrongdoing can even lead to pain in the form of sadness and depression, leading to a downward spiral of further transgressions and pain.

Have you ever tasted something super hot and burned your tongue in the process? At first, it throbs with pain, but then it's numb, and you can't taste anything. Just like you can burn your tongue, your sixth sense can also become numb. Those who continually commit wrongdoings, pushing through the guilt and the throbbing pain of the sixth sense, end up on the most adverse life trail of all. When their sixth sense goes numb or is burned from continued malicious wrongdoings, they continue to escalate into a vortex of actions and decisions with dire repercussions.

I believe that blame pointed toward oneself can be a tool for change and growth. It's the catalyst for the perfect storm. Guilt prevents us from slandering others, from procrastinating for an upcoming assignment, and from skipping the gym.

The happiest and most successful people in the world use their sixth sense the most. Many of these people have called guilt the "voice in their head telling them to do something with their life." Successful people claim that their sixth sense helps them to live blameless lives filled with morality, happiness, and contentment. When they do feel guilt, they see it as an "inner stop-sign" to getting back on track.

On the journey of life to point B, we invariably end up getting distracted and veering off the right path. Remember, **there**

is no being perfect. By embracing our inner guilt as a way to get back on our line and to correct our mistakes, we can avoid paths paved with unhappiness, unfulfillment, pathways which lead to dark caves.

People who regularly commit immoral acts, regardless of their faith, understand and know that what they are doing is wrong. They are the most unhappy of all people.

There are easy ways to avoid guilt. Simple examples include volunteering, smiling at others, helping those in need, complimenting others, and being thankful on an everyday basis. I don't need to belabor the point - **you already know *how* to live a guilt-free life**. So embrace the sixth sense, self-evaluate, and make the decision to fix the areas of your life that are causing you guilt.

Sit Down, Be Humble

A friend of mine told a compelling story in his graduation speech. The story went something like this:

A man who worked long hours and had little money looked outside the window of his house and saw a homeless man. He thought to himself, "At least I have a place to live." The homeless man saw a man limping down the street. He thought to himself, "At least I'm not injured." The limping man looked into an alley and saw a crazy man muttering strange things to himself. He thought to himself, "At least I'm sane." The insane man saw an ambulance drive through the alley. He thought to himself, "At least I'm not sick." When the sick man arrived at the hospital, he saw a body with a black sheet over it. He thought to himself, "At least I'm alive." The dead man had no words to say.

Sometimes we forget what it is we have. We forget how

privileged we are to be where we are, regardless of the circumstances. Often, we even fail to remember those who have helped us along our journey up the mountain.

It doesn't matter how much talent you or anyone has. When you lose sight of how fortunate you are, you immediately put yourself on the path toward a cave. If you aspire to be something - to be great in any way - then heed the wisdom of John Dickson in his book *Humilitas*, in which he proclaims that "Humility makes the great even greater."

Dickson uses inspiring stories, historical examples, and a variety of research to prove his central thesis: "The most influential and inspiring people are often marked by humility."

I will soon provide several inspiring examples of people who exemplify the greatness that comes with this "humility." Still, first, it is worth identifying and noting what humility is in the journey up the mountain.

Humility is remembering the struggles of the journey which made your achievements possible. It doesn't matter where you are in your life journey, it's recognizing and remembering the times of pain, suffering, embarrassment, and the like. Willingly admitting that your achievements are a *result* of your struggles is the first step to becoming humble. Remember that without experiencing the turmoil of the caves, you would lack the developed stamina and strength to make it to the peak. The second step to becoming humble is reaching out and helping others through the hard points of their journey. There is much to be said about this characteristic, but instead, I will spare you the details and let three "Rags to Riches" stories show what humility is.

◆ ◆ ◆

Stubborn Fool #5

John D. Rockefeller was born into an impoverished family

in upstate New York, 1839. His father frequently left him and his mother alone to fend for themselves. Despite this, Rockefeller believed that God had big plans for his future. Becoming an assistant bookkeeper at age six, Rockefeller quickly rose through the ranks and eventually monopolized the oil industry. Although he is said to be the wealthiest American of all time, he was nonetheless an active member of his Baptist Mission Church, rooted by his deep faith. Attributing his success to God, Rockefeller displayed his humanitarian values throughout his life. He was known for throwing dimes to adults and nickels to children wherever he went. As he gave more money, he noticed that he received more. Throughout his life, Rockefeller donated $550 million.

Stubborn Fool #6

Dr. Ben Carson was born in Detroit, Michigan, in 1951. At the age of eight, his father walked out on his family. Living with a psychotic mother, he dealt with adversity throughout his childhood. With overwhelming humility and faith in God, he overcame anger issues, a learning disability, and constant racial discrimination. Despite his hurdles, he graduated near the top of his high school JROTC class and received a scholarship to Yale. He later attended medical school and became the head of neurosurgery at Johns Hopkins by the age of 34. From there, he went on to perform miracle surgeries.

From a young age, Ben's mother, despite her neurological instability, instilled a work ethic in her son like none other. In his autobiography, *Gifted Hands*, Dr. Carson states,

> *"Success is determined not by whether or not you face obstacles, but by your reactions to them. And if you look at these obstacles as a containing fence, they become your excuse for failure. If you look at them as a hurdle, each one strengthens you for the next."*

"Happiness doesn't result from what we get... but what we give."

Stubborn Fool #7

In 1951, Richard Desmond was born into a Jewish family in Hampstead, London. At 11, his parents divorced, forcing him and his mother to move into a less than modest flat above a garage. As a youth, he described himself as lonely and fat. At 14, he quit school to focus on his drumming skills, humbly working as a coat-checker to make ends meet. At 21, he founded a monthly magazine for musicians. Working hard and long hours, he managed to expand his magazine empire to an international level. With the money he earned, he leveraged himself as an avid philanthropist - his net worth was well over $2.5 Billion.

The diffidence displayed in Rockefeller, Carson, and Desmond can be applied to anyone's life. **Humility is a choice**. Although each of the above successes came from modest beginnings and dealt with adversity throughout their youth, they remained humble and worked harder than their competition. They sacrificed accolades for service. Each of them valued giving to others more than receiving recognition. Ultimately, their selfless service allowed them to receive more than they could have ever imagined.

Once embraced, humility will move you up the stairs of success much quicker than you ever could have imagined.

TEN-FINDING ONE'S CALLING

"Most enjoyable activities are not natural; they demand an effort that initially one is reluctant to make. But once the interaction starts to provide feedback to the person's skills, it usually begins to be intrinsically rewarding." - Mihaly Csikszentmihalyi

Imagine a world in which every single person reached their maximum potential. Most humans would likely be far beyond the realm of earth. Medical prodigies would have made the reality of living for hundreds of years a certainty, freshwater would have become an infinite resource, and every individual on the planet would be highly motivated (to the point of madness) to reach their potential. Everyone would be so motivated to achieve their dreams that they would be willing to fail hundreds of times to succeed. Almost everyone would have a niche in society. There would be no suicide rate, less conflict, and increased worldwide productivity.

Okay, back to reality. Only a select group of individuals on this planet reach anywhere close to their maximum potential. I'm referring to the Steve Jobs', Bill Gates', and Elon Musks' of this world. According to Forbes magazine, only the top 1% of the American population controls 43% of the wealth. The three mentioned above are essentially worth 70 times as much as the other 99% of America.

Some might say that this is due to flaws in the system. However, the reality is, not everybody has the tenacity to sustain a *lifestyle* of hard work, sacrifice, and taking chances. Not everyone can quickly figure out their calling and harness their energy towards it. Not everybody chooses to live a pure, driven, and wholehearted life.

Still, it is becoming more accessible and easier to succeed in a nation where a lack of motivation and a sudden increase in crime is noticeable, especially among Millenials and youth. A *DoSomething.org* article featuring high school dropout rates claims that every year, 1.2 million students drop out of high school, and 25% of first-year high school students fail to graduate high school on time. Statistics show that a high school dropout will end up making $200,000 less than a high school graduate and a more significant $1,000,000 less than a college graduate over his or her lifetime. Studies have also shown that these same high school dropouts end up committing about 75% of crimes within the United States.

My experiences and research reveal that motivation is essential to achievement of any kind. The effective drive must be intrinsic. For example, the successful scholar does not generally read on their own time because they want to achieve a certain GPA. Instead, they read independently for their love of learning and personal growth. Most accomplished medical researchers don't experiment in order to accumulate personal net worth. Instead, they seek the satisfaction of curing the disease or learning about the subject in question. They do it so that their contributions might benefit others one day. Most accomplished professionals, whatever it is that they do, possess a true intrinsic passion for the cause they represent.

Military schools, modeled after the United States military, have perfected the process of training and developing cadets into motivated and independent young men and women ready to become an integral part of society. This model enhances and promotes values along with respect - essential characteristics necessary to build discipline within the cadet. Military school training guides students to discover their true potential and develop a clear vision for their lives, whether it be in their field of study, profession, or later in life.

At the end of my junior year, I perused the school lunchroom, surveying different students asking them what they sought to do with their future. Most of the students had a clear vision and direction mapped out. I got responses such as, "I want to be a physician," or, "I want to be a builder," or "I want to pursue an accounting degree to start a business someday." Of the approximate 100 students I surveyed, only 10% were unable to express what they wanted to do with their life definitively.

80% of students in the United States end up changing their major at least once, according to the National Center for Education Statistics. In contrast, the majority of military school students have their hearts set on their passions as early as middle school!

What is it about these students that separate them from their peers in public school?

It's simple. cadets are encouraged to set goals and achieve them. They do this through a structured, disciplined, daily routine. Such a schedule doesn't allow students much time for horseplay. The following exemplifies a typical daily schedule at my school.

    0630 - Wake Up
    0630 - 0700 - Clean Rooms for 0700 Inspection
    0730 - 0805 - Breakfast
    0810 - 1230 - Morning Classes
    1235 - 1325 - Formation and Lunch
    1330 - 1500 - Afternoon Classes and Teacher Help

1500 - 1600 - "Company" Time
1600 - 1800 - Sports
1800 - 1915 - Dinner
1930 - 2130 - Study Hours
2130 - 2200 - Hygiene
2200 - Lights Out

One can see that little "free time" exists for cadets to roam free and that every time of the day has a specific purpose. For example, study hours are for studying, hygiene time is for showering, and formation is for company accountability.

At first, I absolutely loathed the routine schedule. I wanted to do what I wanted to do when I wanted to do it!

However, the structured schedule taught me two fundamental principles. The first is that amid the havoc of the world, every day must feed into a purpose. The second is to approach each day as if it were your last.

"Singleness of purpose is one of the chief essentials for success in life, no matter what may be one's aim." -John D. Rockefeller

ELEVEN-ADOLF CHAUFF, YES MR. CORRECTIONAL OFFICER

In 1973, psychologist Philip Zimbardo set up a mock prison in order to conduct the Stanford Prison Experiment. He selected 23 student volunteers to participate and split them up into two randomized groups - prisoners and guards.

The experiment itself would simulate an actual prison. First, the "prisoners" were arrested at their homes, taken to the police station, and fingerprinted. They were then blindfolded and brought to the mock prison in the Stanford University Psychology Department, where they were stripped naked and issued a prison uniform and ID number by the "guards." White walls, small cells, and prison-like doors and windows made the simulation prison seem almost too real for said "experiment."

Although chosen randomly, guards were reasoned with that they were chosen "for a purpose." They were told they had to maintain order in prison by any means necessary without using physical force. Throughout the experiment, Zimbardo would oversee the prison and act as a "prison warden."

Early on in the experiment, the guards overstepped their

authority. At 2:30 a.m. on the first night, they brutally awoke the prisoners with piercing sounds of whistles and forced them to "recount" their numbers in front of their cells. When some wouldn't count loud enough, they were forced by the guards to do pushups and other physically exerting tasks.

On day two, to the surprise of the guards, the prisoners revolted by removing their prison uniforms, ripping off their numbers, and locking themselves in their prison cells. In response, the guards used a fire extinguisher to force the hostile prisoners away from the prison cell doors.

When back in control, the guards asserted even more dominance than before. As the guards became increasingly strict and abusive, the prisoners became submissive out of fear and dependency. There were varied forms of atrocities committed. Guards threw prisoners' blankets in the dirt, denied prisoners food, water, and sleep, and put bags over the prisoners' heads. They forced the prisoners to march around the prison, chained prisoners' legs, forced prisoners to clean toilets with their bare hands, and coerced prisoners into performing lewd dances with other prisoners. As if this madness weren't enough, prisoners were referred to by their assigned "prisoner numbers" and had to address the guards as "Mr. Correctional Officer."

After just a few days of this repeated maltreatment, most prisoners began to believe they were, in reality, prisoners, and some began to lose their minds. Only three days into the experiment, prisoner #8612 had a mental breakdown. Despite his collapse, he was denied "leave" from the prison. Only until he screamed deliriously for hours was he then allowed to leave. Later, when an "interventional priest" was brought in to talk to the prisoners, each of them introduced themselves by their assigned prison number instead of by their name. Furthermore, prisoner #819 broke down in tears after the priest told him he needed a lawyer to leave the prison.

The experiment was meant to last for two weeks. It spiraled out of control and thus came to a halting end after only six days. An excerpt from Zimbardo's interview with a correctional officer gives vivid insight into prisoner-guard interactions.

> "...during the inspection I went to Cell Two to mess up a bed which a prisoner had just made, and he grabbed me, screaming that he had just made it and that he was not going to let me mess it up. He grabbed me by the throat, and although he was laughing, I was pretty scared. I lashed out with my stick and hit him on the chin, although not very hard, and when I freed myself, I became angry."

In comparing the two, the guards were no different than the prisoners. However, when given a false sense of power, and when put in the right environment, the guards abused their power. The most abusive guards even admitted that they could have never imagined themselves committing such egregious acts as they did during the experiment.

Interestingly enough, it took only hours for these seemingly ordinary students to assume the roles of abusive prison guards or correctional officers. Similarly, we, too, have the propensity to become like those correctional officers, forcing prisoners to spew out their assigned numbers to our satisfaction.

Any leader can abuse their power. We see it throughout history; we've seen it with kings, dictators, ambassadors, ministry leaders, CEOs, managers, police officers, and yes, even officers in the military. I came to a deeper understanding of this phenomenon after I committed this vile act. When placed in a position of authority, I assumed the role of a correctional officer, fortunately, not to the same extent as in the Stanford Prison Experiment. You'll see that my harsh attitude to my subordinates and my micromanagement were detrimental. Allow me to introduce myself: Mr. Correctional Officer, or First Sergeant Chauff.

Correctional officers have authority over prisoners. They don't ask the prisoners for help, nor do they delegate responsibility to them. They certainly are not there to build a team of prisoners. Correctional officers are mainly concerned about performing their "role" - keeping their subordinates in line. They have no concern about hurting a prisoner's feelings. It's laughable to think they would listen to a prisoner's suggestions, let alone be their friend.

The president of the United States is physically incapable of approaching the citizens of every single family in this country for suggestions on how to improve it. (He couldn't possibly have enough time to read each Twitter comment). Instead, the president has an organized hierarchy of leaders that assist and deliver to him information from lower echelons of "command."

Similarly, correctional officers do not realize that one leader, guard, dictator, or manager does not have the intelligence, time, and overall wisdom to manage every trivial detail within their jurisdiction. Correctional officers have the potential to be abusive micromanagers. That's what I had become my junior year as I assumed the role of First Sergeant. I was responsible for the training, mentoring, discipline, accountability, room cleanliness, military training, academic well-being, and physical fitness of the forty cadets in Alpha Company. It was too much responsibility for just one person to manage on their own.

Early on, I thought I was more than competent to micromanage all forty students and bring the company to perfection. As you already know, the rooms had to be clean. I didn't just require rooms to be clean, that wasn't enough. I expected my company's rooms to be at Din's standards - especially the beds. Each morning, I proudly marched from room to room, itching to tell the cadets what was below standard in their rooms.

"Fix this, make your bed, redo it!" I spoke with authority. "Ten, nine, eight, seven...six...," I shouted during roll-call.

I scoured the rooms yelling angrily throughout the hallway, looking for cadets who didn't come out during my countdown from ten to zero. During study hours, I would walk around from one room to the next, making cadets study and forcing them to do so in the hallways as punishment for poor grades. Even during hygiene, I made sure all forty cadets showered, every... single... night.

When a cadet didn't live up to my standards, I corrected them on the spot and quickly pointed out their mistakes to the rest of the company. I never allowed for feedback from my tired and weary cadets - what could they possibly have to offer me?

Like in the Stanford Prison Experiment, authoritarian micromanagement worked initially. For the first week, my cadets were exceptionally squared away - their rooms were clean, their uniforms immaculate, and they were punctual. Just like in prison, everyone initially did as they were told. However, this was achieved at a price. Like the prison guards, I always felt guilty, tired, and moody. This led to sleepless nights and yelling at cadets. I often barked at students to fix their uniforms. I berated cadets when they were late to formation. I replaced the little free time available with cumbersome tasks like directing cadets to shine their floors, make their beds, and organize their closets to perfection.

Like in the prison experiment, my superiors told me I was doing a good job "assuming my role." However, my subordinates could see that I was more concerned about forcing them to meet my standards than about their improvement and welfare. One evening as I roamed the hallways checking for cadets on their phones, I overheard someone say "Adolf Chauff." What? I couldn't believe what I just heard. It was like someone knocked the wind out of me! With pride and disbelief, I stomped back to my room and cried. I was ashamed and oblivious of my leadership. "Adolf Chauff" sounded even worse than Mr. Correctional Officer. Was I that bad?

Upon reflection, I realized that I was running things into the ground. I had two platoon sergeants, two platoon leaders, six squad leaders, and a company commander who were there to help me. 11 leaders at my disposal could have readily and gladly helped me manage the company. I had tricked myself into doing their jobs so that things could be done "my way." I had become a control freak who tolerated nothing less than perfection. I was a Correctional Officer! I only cared about the **company's** success - not improving the **individuals**.

I continued. During week two of micromanagement, my body was approaching its limit. When I got out of bed, my arms, legs, and head told me, "**NO!**" I ignored it and eventually became sick. Midway through week three, I hit a wall. One morning, I woke up with my head pounding and my throat throbbing. My toothbrush fell out of my limp hand onto the ground as I attempted to brush my teeth. My muscles ached to the point where I had difficulty putting on my uniform, and finally, my raspy voice was gone. I was completely useless. I couldn't get through another day on my own.

With a struggling whisper, I brought my leaders to my room. Usually, I worked without them, but I desperately needed them now. I told them that I would need their help in the morning. I could see the awakening excitement in their eyes - they would finally get a chance to work with their cadets outside of my iron grip.

"First [and Second] platoons outside in front of your rooms," my platoon sergeants called in their sections of the hallway, "5.....4.....3.....2.....1.....0!" To my surprise, every single cadet in each platoon came into the hall. "Amazing," I thought.

I was still sure that nothing would get done beyond that. It didn't matter - I didn't have the energy to be a correctional officer. However, within seconds, squad leaders were bustling through the rooms of their squad members, encouraging them to clean. Ten minutes later, the quarters of all the cadets in the company were spotless. As I limped into rooms, I looked for beds that weren't up to Din's standards. I looked for disheveled blinds. I looked for books that were not flush against the edge of the shelf. How strange, I thought. There was nothing! I was sure

I'd find something. To my dismay, everyone and everything was in its place.

Eight hours later, following class, my body crashed, and I blacked out in my bed. "**Do not disturb 1SGT. Work-related sickness.**" read the post-it note on the smudged window of my door. It hung there for the next week. As the cadets in my company walked by, they were confused. Many of them wondered if they could coast since "Adolf Chauff" was MIA. Remember the famous jingle from the movie, *The Wizard of Oz* that went like this? "Ding dong the witch is dead the witch is dead the witch is dead, ding dong the wicked witch is dead!!" I rest my case.

My sickness marked the end of my career as a micromanager. I decided to gladly hang up my hat as "Adolf Chauff, Mr. Correctional Officer." After recovering, I sought to practice real leadership - the kind that motivated people and built a team - not the guidance that degraded others and decreased morale. I realized I needed to give up complete control and contentment of knowing that everyone was doing exactly what I wanted them to do when I wanted them to do it. I did a significant disservice to those I was over.

I did a complete turnaround and changed my approach. Instead of controlling everything and everyone, I began to trust the leaders within my company. For week one of my "step back," my company was not where I would have wanted it. I still found the occasional sock on the floor during room inspections, an unshaven cadet, or stain on a uniform. Nonetheless, the thought of going back to my old style of leadership was no longer an option.

In the next month, I implemented changes in my leadership approach which drastically improved morale, company level of performance, and team solidarity. In doing so, I solidified three leadership attributes which I believe make for superlative figureheads in any situation.

First, an effective leader must be **humble**. Humility is defined as "the quality of having a modest or low view of one's importance." Therefore, the leader values the individuals of a given team over themselves. I found that students were much more apt to listen to what I had to say as I became approachable and sincerely took an interest in them. I made a conscious effort to put their needs above my own. Why? Because humility is the bridge of trust between a leader and those they oversee. I've found that Dickson's words resonate this truth:

> *"When people trust us, they tend to believe what we say, and few are considered more trustworthy than those who choose to use their power for the good of others above themselves."*

I chose to sit with the students in my company at lunch, getting to know them instead of sitting with my buddies. I found out that one student from Mexico used to play competitive Rugby! I made a conscious effort to spend time doing what my cadets wanted to do, such as playing Pub-G (I could care less about video games, especially games related to my brother's favorite game - Fortnite) on the weekends. Instead of yelling at students when disrespected, I would pull them aside and share embarrassing stories about my earlier years as an unruly cadet. I also began walking around the dorms, checking up on how my cadets were doing rather than scolding them for their shortcomings. I started to care - really care. One evening as I stumbled onto a room full of cadets, I asked: "How is everyone?" An echo boomeranged back, "fine First Sergeant!" I caught a glimpse of an individual who wiped what looked like tears from his eyes.

"No, really, how is everyone?" I asserted in a more friendly tone than usual. Later that night, I finally got it - I understood the importance of approachability and humility as I sat with one of the students in my room, comforting him over his mother's death and the overwhelming problems he was having with his brother.

It's by **example** that a leader motivates team members to thrive collectively. Not only does a leader represent precisely what they want their people to become, but rewards those who excel in doing so. Leaders are to be the hardest workers of everyone, the most motivated and inspired. At St. John's, leaders have the best rooms and uniforms in the company, leaders wake up before their cadets and go to bed after them, and leaders help their cadets improve their grades as they excel in theirs.

By being that example, no-one was able to dispute what I had to say. I proved to my cadets that I would never make them do anything that I, as a leader, was not willing to do. Unfortunately, that meant occasionally taking out the trash, mopping the hallway, picking up banana peels in the bathroom, and yes, even unclogging a toilet on a Saturday.

Instead of fitting into a "role," a leader **shapes his or her role**. That, I believe, distinguishes good leaders from exceptional leaders. Does the Correctional Officer have to be harsh to prisoners? Does the company CEO have to yell at employees to command respect? Does the first sergeant need to act tough and unapproachable in order to run a company of cadets? Exceptional leaders understand that the answers to these questions vary according to each individual.

Furthermore, leaders question the "why" behind the traditional tasks in their role. "Why do we do things this way," they ask, "Are there ways that we can make this more efficient or better for employees?" They don't accept the proverbial response of, "this is just how it's always been done." No, indeed, they find a better way, and they "own the role."

I stopped yelling. I stopped micromanaging. I became inclusive of my leaders, involving them in my plans and decisions. I became a mentor to each cadet in my company - almost like I would my brother. My cadets started coming to my room and freely sharing their thoughts and issues with me - almost as if I were the company counselor in addition to the First Sergeant. I also became known for my catchy one-liners. "It's going to be a great day at St. John's Northwestern Military Academy," I would holler throughout the hallways. Sound familiar? "Are we having fun yet?" I would lead with before commanding formation. "Each of you is going to be something awesome one day," I would tell my cadets as they stood straight as pencils for platoon room inspections. At least once a week, I showed my company a motivational video. (When it comes to motivation, nobody inspires me more than David Goggins). I created a "platoon competition" - a way that the two platoons made up of 20 cadets each, could compete in room inspections, grades, discipline, and military drill. At the start of being the first sergeant, I earned the name "Adolf Chauff." Two and a half months later, I proved that being an excellent first sergeant could be done without yelling and intimidation but rather with sincerity and devotion.

The night I was scheduled to move out of the company, I decided to hold a meeting. When I informed my cadets that they would be getting a new first sergeant, the room suddenly broke into tears. I was in shock. Students came up to hug me, to thank me, and some to even cry on my shoulder. I was overwhelmed with emotion. I found myself reciprocating with tears of endearment. I didn't realize how close I had grown to my cadets - to my little brothers.

Through humility, I discovered a new heartfelt approach - yelling was unnecessary - cadets wanted to listen to me out of respect for me. Through exemplifying authentic leadership, I was amazed to find cadets regularly trying to emulate me. Through developing my role, I discovered that "owning it" is more effective than trying to fit into the status quo or "the way things have always been done." Just like that, I went from "Adolf Chauff, Mr. Correctional Officer," to almost a "big brother for 40 students."

Anyone can enhance themselves as a leader, in any situation, by employing **humility, example,** and by **shaping their role.** It requires more work and heart than leading by sheer dictatorship. The rewards, however, are immeasurable.

TWELVE-IT'S THE JOURNEY, NOT THE DESTINATION

"If the journey to success and happiness was a hundred miles, some people would calculate it by meters and get discouraged by the numbers they come up with." - Edmond Mbiaka

It's almost too often that we hear of world-class athletes, musicians, and celebrities overdosing or committing suicide. How is it that they are unhappy with everything they have? It's unfathomable to understand why one would end their life with accolades a mile long. It's because their journey to the top of their mountain was reached without much of a fight. Their success does not correspond to their happiness.

I love the movie *A Star Is Born.* I want to discuss one of the main characters in particular - Jackson Maine. Jackson is a famous country music singer who eventually falls into a negative spiral. He has everything that anyone could ever want or imagine: fame, fortune, fans, and finally, love. However, Jackson manages his stress by drinking and taking painkillers religiously before his performances. As Jackson descends into his spiral of addiction, he begins to lose fans, fame, and reputation.

One night, Jackson passes out drunk in public. Waking up on the street, his friend, Noodles, allows him to recover in his nearby house. Noodles, the loyal friend that he is, proceeds to give Jackson insightful advice.

> *"You know it's like, I dunno you.... You float out... float out at sea, then one day you find a port and say, 'I'm gonna stay here for a few days.' A few days becomes a few years. Then you forget where you're going in the first place. Then you realize you don't really give a shit about where you were going, cause you like where you at."*

Jackson liked where he was at. He had fame, fortune, and love. What he didn't realize, however, was that his addiction, a byproduct of his insecurities, was destroying his life. It wasn't until a fateful day when he wet himself on stage at the Grammys standing next to his beautiful, devoted wife that he started to take his addiction seriously. But in the end, he hangs himself.

So, what equates to happiness? It appeared as though Jackson had it all. After seeing hundreds of students and reading about the happiest and unhappiest people earth, I've discovered that sustained happiness does not come from success itself. Happiness comes from the journey. Take, for instance, the Navy SEALs These soldiers have endured the most arduous journey that the world has to offer - around 50 weeks of continuous, rigorous military training.

"On your feet, maggots!" barks a Navy SEAL instructor.

A smile suddenly appears on the instructor's face as he watches the group of fifty potential SEALs link arms and struggle to stand up in the bone-chilling, ocean water. The sun has yet to rise. The SEALs are thrilled to get their sore bottoms off of the sand and their chests out of the waist-deep, rough waters. After a mile of lunges, anything at this point seems like a piece of cake.

The SEAL instructor tilts his hat. "Today, you will need to execute a 500-yard swim in nine minutes or less, 90 or more push-ups in two minutes or less, 90 or more sit-ups in two minutes or less, 18 pull-ups, and a 1.5 mile run in combat boots in 9.5 min or less. Oh, and there will be only two minutes of rest in-between events! If you don't qualify, you will be removed from training."

Another instructor with a tattoo of the SEAL trident on his bulging right bicep interrupts. "Those who pass will join arms and run into the 40-degree ocean to swim two miles across the bay with fins. Life vests will not be provided."

Tilted hat rolls up his sleeves, oblivious to the 45 mph winds. "Gentlemen, if the swim is completed in passing time, you'll be introduced again to Iron Mike later tonight."

Bulging bicep cuts to the chase. "Otherwise, you'll be eating sugar cookies and rolling with the logs in the sand before lunch."

Tilted hat gives the potential SEALs a movie-like salute and a half-hearted smile. "All you have to do is ring the bell if you want to have a hot chocolate and go back home to mommy. See you at lunch, boys."

The would-be-hopefuls knew the truth. There was no passing, and there was no escaping the sugar cookies. The reality was, they would all be sitting at lunch with sand in their armpits, hair, and food. There was no time for complaining. They could save it for next week - Hell Week. Five days and five nights with a deprived four hours of sleep each night. Regardless, most of the SEALs were prepared to die before they'd ring that bell. Only quitters rang the bell.

Every year, 40,000 people express interest in becoming a Navy SEAL - a very esteemed, highly trained, and coveted group. Who wouldn't want to be part of the highly-trained unit that killed Osama Bin Laden in his bunker and rescued Captain Phillips from Somali pirates? Of those who pursue this dream, only six percent, or about 1,000 recruits, are permitted to enter this rigorous training. Only 25% of those recruits make it through the program. The approximately 250 SEALs who complete the program are arguably some of the most mentally and physically fit human beings on the planet.

> *My strength didn't come from lifting weights. My strength came from lifting myself up every time I was knocked down. - SEAL Recruit*

> *Pain is weakness leaving the body. - Navy SEALs*

> *Instead of thinking about the entire six month course, the week's training schedule or even the daily schedule, many trainees focus on literally getting by one small event at a time, be it getting dressed, eating breakfast, running to the obstacle course, completing the obstacle course within standards, etc. - the focus is one successive microevolution or time frame. - SEAL Instructor*

> *It takes discipline to focus only on high-value targets instead of giving in to the temptation of the low hanging fruit life serves up daily." - Mark Divine*

    Each SEAL understands the joy that comes from overcoming obstacles. They also understand that their mental and physical grit are developed during their journey, making any victory all the sweeter.

I've found that so many people go through their lives so focused on a destination that they don't pay enough attention to their journey! While working toward a destination is essential, the mission is what matters most.

One highly esteemed Navy SEAL who can explain this principal with conviction is David Goggins. Goggins' message has had a forceful impact on my life and the lives of many others. While I feel that I could write an entire book about Goggins from watching his hundreds of motivational videos, I'll instead have to refer you to his bestselling book, *Can't Hurt Me*.

Goggins' peaks going up his life mountain include passing the ASVAB to get into the military, completing Navy SEAL training and Ranger School, placing third in the Badwater 130 (a 130-mile race through the scorching heat of Death Valley), and setting a world record for the most pull-ups in 24 hours.

It's important to note, Goggins didn't acquire these great revelations when he crossed the finish line of any race or met any of his goals. Goggins didn't suddenly become great when he was named the "toughest man in the world." He indeed didn't find happiness when at the peak of any of his mountains. Where Goggins found joy, success, self-improvement, and peace was during his journey - amidst challenges. Goggins' wisdom serves to show that success isn't a destination, but rather a lifestyle of pushing through challenges. As you read on, Goggins' knowledge displayed below, is life-changing:

"The only way you are ever going to get to the other side of this journey is that you have to suffer. To grow, you must suffer."

"When you think you are done, you are into 40% of what your body is capable of doing."

"The best lessons learned didn't come from a book. They came from me seeing things through to the end."

"A lot of us don't know about another world that exists for us because it's on the other side of suffering. That's the real growth in life."

"You can't live your life being afraid to fail. All of those failures made me the success I am today. Stay hard. Stay in the fight."

Goggins isn't superhuman. He's a normal human being like you and me, a person all too familiar with adversity. In his own words, "I was called nigger every day of my life" growing up. Goggins also suffered physical and mental abuse repeatedly from his father.

Goggins started at base camp as an Ecolab worker exterminating cockroaches, making $1,000 a month. At 297 lbs, after finishing a box of donuts one morning, he saw Navy SEALs ringing the bell on television. Goggins saw himself as a bell ringer, one who was living within a box of mediocrity.

Disgusted with his life, he decided to embrace suffering and turn his life around for the better by starting his journey up the mountain. He quit his job and consulted with a local naval recruiter. He was informed he would need to lose 106 lbs in two months to even qualify for SEAL training. All but one of his recruiters said he couldn't do it. On his first day of training, Goggins failed to run more than half a mile, yet he pressed on and eventually qualified for the coveted SEAL training. *That is success.* During his training, Goggins endured and persevered despite having to start over twice due to injury. *That* is success. Later on, to achieve the 24-hour pull-up record, Goggins had to complete over 70,000 pullups in training. He failed twice, yet he endured. *That* is success. I would call Goggins one of our "stubborn fools" when he says the following.

> *"You have to be willing to fail 1,000 times to succeed and be willing to repeat that the rest of your life. Don't overthink it! Just get after it!"*

During times of suffering, persistent hikers must use self-talk and *internal* motivation to push through negative emotions, fatigue, and discouragement. It's a similar kind of affirmation that keeps SEALs going: to finish those last ten pull-ups; to continue SEAL training and run into 45-degree ocean; to help their team carry the massive log for another five exhausting miles; to become the best version of themselves. For SEALs like Goggins, the why for the journey entails getting on the right track and proving everyone wrong who ever doubted him. "Everybody comes to a point in their life when they want to quit." Goggins asserts, "It's what you do at that moment that determines who you are." Imagine where your life would be if, for the next five years, you chose to endure every single time you wanted to quit.

Don't take this too far. Like so many lonely hikers, I was once consumed with reaching the summit of my journey that I continually felt burnt out. This constant feeling made me believe that I would never have the energy to make it to the top of the mountain. I didn't care about my journey enough to conserve energy for it, but instead consistently ran myself into the ground to reach my destination.

Goggins helped me to see that success, happiness, and fulfillment are found in the journey - not at the destination. Success goes hand in hand with perseverance - continuing on my mission despite the odds, despite my lack of intelligence, and despite those who tell me I can't do it. For me, success and fulfillment are no longer about getting into a stellar college. Success, satisfaction, and happiness come from putting everything I have into the journey towards any of my destinations. **Are we having fun yet?**

I can't even begin to explain the satisfied, fulfilled feeling you'll experience at the end of the day when you know you gave your very best and you didn't hold back. After all, you can only do your best! When you exert your optimum, it no longer leaves room for fretting. You begin to realize that putting all of your energy into your journey is more rewarding than reaching your destination. That's worth repeating.

Putting all of your energy into your journey is more rewarding than reaching your destination.

In contrast, when you haven't given your best, and you've held back, your psyche is aware, and you are left feeling discouraged and depressed. You then worry and obsess about your destination. You become uneasy and forget about your journey. At times while writing this book, I was concerned about who might read it, and whether they'd like it. Once I pushed those worries aside and gave up fretting about the destination, my most meaningful writing came to fruition.

How Others May Perceive Your Effort and Self-Improvement

Driving home for spring Break, junior year, I was spent. I was tired. I was in the cave. On the wall of the cave were lies I kept telling myself. "I deserve better. I can relax while I'm on break. I'm going to let go for a while." I bought into it too. I was convinced that a party would allow me to escape from the struggles of my journey for a night. I truly believed at that moment that "living it up" over Spring break would get me out of my cave.

So I proceeded to hit up some of my friends to go to a party. We arrived at 9:00 p.m. In the living room, I saw many of my old school friends from seventh grade. All of them were surprised to see me, barraging me with questions. "Did you go to war?" people asked me (Seriously, dude - I was only 16!), "Do they make you shoot guns on the weekends?" (Are you kidding me?) "Why did you choose to go there?" Let the fun begin...

I was no stranger to these questions. "Military school has been perfect for me," I replied. My old school-mates in the crowd frowned. I noticed a few eye rolls amidst the interrogation.

A girl spewed, "So you chose to go?"

"I did, sort of..." I replied. More frowns.

I escaped that conversation as quickly as I could. There was no need for explaining myself - people didn't understand. How could they? How could most people understand that "Military School" was different from what was portrayed in *American Sniper, Lone Survivor, Black Hawk Down,* and *The Perfect School* episode of *Goosebumps*?

I made my way around trying to reconnect with some of my old buddies - those I used to goof off with in seventh grade. I ran into the friend that used to make computer-animated button noises with me in the back of history class. Likewise, I encountered the friends I went to the principal's office with in an attempt to "fire" my old English teacher and even some of the people in the class who laughed when I called 9-1-1 on the school phone in fifth grade. No matter who I conversed with, I felt out of place. There was a noticeable lack of connection. At times, the deafening silence and awkward pauses confirmed that what I once had with my old buddies was now strained. I'm not blaming anyone - it just was. I continued to care about my old friends, but it became evident that time, distance, and experiences put us on different paths. There was a difference between the brotherhood of my military school friends and my friends from back home. Make no mistake, I was included in all their outings upon return. They never left me out. However, the comradery was lacking. Regardless, I continued forward, ignoring what I felt gnawing inside. Many a time, I longed to talk about their futures and reflect on my fears and trepidations. Instead, the conversation was usually shallow.

Almost everyone I spoke with was the same - it was as if time stood still. In most cases, there was no change since I had seen them four years earlier. When I asked some of my old friends what they aspired to do in college or for their future, responses were generally, "What do you mean, man?" or "Nah, I'm not worried about that."

Something was different. Don't get me wrong, I had nothing against anyone. It was a fun crowd. I didn't see myself as better than anyone - just different. I quickly figured out that I didn't belong there, or any party for that matter. Despite the voices in my head urging me to leave, I stayed.

I can recall a similar situation where I somehow managed to put myself in the center of yet another group dialogue. In the conversation, one of my friends mentioned they had given a gift to their younger sibling for their birthday. So I asked, "Like a monetary gift?" (Okay, give me a break. I had been studying SAT vocabulary for the week prior). The comment brought dead silence, then laughter.

Back to the party, as I was talking to a group of friends, I suddenly felt drool on my arm. A drunken girl was now trying to come lean on me. Everybody started laughing as she collapsed onto the floor with a thud a few seconds later.

Then I heard some whispering in the near distance, "Pfff, military school. Why does he stand up so straight?"

I nodded my head a few times and went upstairs. I looked at myself in the mirror and wondered what I was doing there. I never felt so out of place. I felt like a "fish out of water." It felt as if I were microscopically dissected, from the way I walked to my posture to my language. I was hanging onto the past, but in my heart of hearts, I knew I had no business being there.

What was so different about me? I visualized myself back on the mountain. I couldn't find anyone from this party with me. I was looking towards and trekking towards my summits: getting closer to God, getting into a decent college, writing this book, getting a good ACT score, and becoming mentally and physically fit.

As I continued to look at my reflection, I realized what military school had done for me. Many at this party hadn't grown in strength, discipline, or mentality over the past few years. Most were still at basecamp without goals and summits for themselves to reach. From just talking to those around me, I gathered that the highest peak for many of my peers was instant gratification - a hookup or a win in beer pong.

All was not lost; if anything, I gained wisdom from being there.

That night at the party taught me that when you truly begin to change and grow, and when you leave your comfort zone, it *will* make others uncomfortable. Perhaps they will look down on you, criticize you, or slander you. You may be branded as "odd." Some may even feel threatened by your transformation and self-refinement. Once you truly commit to being the best version of you, you'll find that you almost "outgrow" certain friends who don't share in your level of commitment.

In 1545, William Turner termed the phrase "birds of a feather flock together." In nature, he alluded, birds frequently form flocks to guarantee their safety in numbers. Similar to birds, people with parallel interests, hobbies, and levels of commitment flock together to avoid being chastised.

What I've noticed is most lackadaisical people seek the company of other lackadaisical people. Most unmotivated people find the company of other unmotivated folks, and most gossipers seek the company of other gossipers. It makes complete sense.

Just Five People

The Compound Effect is a riveting, energetic, and motivating read. In the book, Darren Hardy caught my attention when he mentioned the research of social psychologist Dr. David McClellan of Harvard. "... [The people you habitually associate with] determine as much as 95% of your success or failure in life."

Here is what that translates to: If the wrong people surround you, then you have a one in 20 chance of ever making it to the peak of any of life's mountains. This isn't a new concept. The bible is quite clear when it states in 1 Corinthians 15:33, "Don't be fooled, bad friends will ruin good habits." In another translation, it says, "Bad company corrupts good character.

It makes sense. The people you associate with, like it or not, are essentially who you emulate. Motivational speaker Jim Rohn affirms this when he states, *"You are the average of the five people you spend the most time with."*

Think about it. If you're unclear about your path to the top of the mountain, doesn't it make sense to at least spend time with a few people who have a clear vision of their ways?

Along your journey, you will encounter many hikers who will *choose* never to make it to the summit; they will stick together to feel better about themselves. Notice, I used the word "choose" because it is precisely that - a choice. In the same way, *you* must choose to separate from those types of hikers.

THIRTEEN-THE MEANING IN RELATIONSHIPS

My mid-afternoon study session was interrupted by two of my close friends - Charlie Robby and Jabin Victor. They wanted to hang out and watch a movie. They *always* knew how to get me out of study mode. Always. Whether it was dangling sour-patch kids in front of my window or claiming that an adult needed to talk to me, they new the hot buttons to press. I was easy prey.

Jabin was the kind of person who was naturally smart. He always knew precisely where effort and work were needed, and exactly how much was required to get by. That's why his "cram sessions" usually started on the day of the exam. I always knew when Jabin had an upcoming exam because his lights (he lived across from me) would burn through my eyes at 4:00 a.m. Then, at breakfast, Jabin would lock into his scribbled notes for whatever class he was studying for. Jabin's idea of a challenge was a bit different from mine. His approach was getting through seven seasons of Game of Thrones in just three weeks. He did it with ease and always managed to ace his college calculus exams during those weeks.

Charlie Robby was a friend who could make me laugh in

any situation. During a chapel service my sophomore year, he was able to derive thirty innuendos from the pastor's sermon, which otherwise had made the rest of the student body fall asleep. At one point, he laughed so hard that he dropped some of his belongings, causing a ruckus and prompting a burst of nervous laughter from yours truly. The president of our academy, just two rows in front of us, became aware of our behavior. Even with him gawking at us, Charlie kept on laughing with me.

"Skyler!" Jabin yelled, "Let's watch Game of Thrones!"

"No, thanks, guys," I responded wearily. "I've got studying to do."

"Dude!" Charlie hollered, "We're graduating next week."

I really did want to hang out with Charlie and Jabin. They were the type of friends that I had fun with but who also cared about my success. Hanging out with them was lighthearted and fun - a time where I could "unwind" and "let go" of the week's stressors.

"I'm studying!" I yelled through the window. "Leave me alone!"

A wave of emotions hit me as I remembered all of the times I said something along these lines. I was now standing at their graduation ceremony wishing I could take back the many times I said "no" to their propositions. As I bid Charlie and Jabin farewell, I realized that I would never get that time back at St. John's. After their final "senior walk," I went to my room and cried. I realized that all the studying in the world could not replace the happiness that true friendship has to offer.

The book *Tuesdays With Morrie* by Mitch Albom is a sad yet inspirational read. The book challenged me on my view of priorities. In this memoir, Mitch watches as his favorite college professor, Morrie, dies of Amyotrophic Lateral Sclerosis. As Morrie's body becomes a "pile of wax," as Albom puts it, his professor remains strong. Through talking to his professor on his deathbed, Mitch realizes life's real priorities. Morrie explains, "Money is not a substitute for tenderness, and power is not a substitute for tenderness. I can tell you, as I'm sitting here dying when you most need it, neither money nor power will give you the feeling you're looking for, no matter how much of them you have."

Nor could a perfect ACT score, in my case. Not any goal accomplished. Not admission into any college. That's where the book sobered me. No matter the amount of success and prosperity one has throughout high school, college, career, or life, they will not achieve true happiness solely by the accolades of their accomplishments. Are you successful if you possess a mansion full of trophies and other accolades, but no friends, family, or spouse to share it with? No, you're just a *lonely* hiker. I learned that the hard way as I said goodbye to the "friends" who I spent less time with for my personal gain.

With that said, and examples to support my theory, I have to challenge the American Dream. While the American Dream is promising with the illusion of being fulfilling, there lies an essential flaw in its nature. The American Dream encourages people to do **whatever necessary** to achieve success. A one-track-mind taken to the extreme could very likely produce this "dream"... but at what cost? It almost puts so many into the nightmare of becoming a *lonely* hiker.

During my sophomore year, although I had attained a high GPA, I was stressed and unhappy. Although I achieved academic honors, I still wanted more. Eventually, more wasn't enough. I yearned to get into my dream colleges. Therefore, I spent entire weekends studying, reading, and taking standardized tests to fill the empty void I felt inside.

Obsession for more leads to burnout. However, having faithful friends while trekking up the mountain will help you push through the off-times. Even Hellen Keller, a woman who was both blind and deaf, learned to understand the power of true friendship.

"I would rather walk with a friend in the dark, than alone in the light." - Hellen Keller

Authentic friends are the warmth during the blizzards, the light at the end of the caves, and the traction preventing you from falling from the mountain. Sincere friends encourage and motivate you to keep going on your journey. It's a relationship that, when reciprocated in this manner, produces growth, trust, and sustenance for most anything.

"If I Can Just Have It... I'll Be Happy!"

I used to be a basket of emotions. I had some talent, but I was disrespectful to the core. I remember how my mother used to say, "I don't care how talented or smart you are, if you don't exhibit respect to those around you, then *you*, my friend, are nothing." I used to think that if only I were smarter, *then* I'd be happy and RESPECTFUL. I would also think that if I could just get that perfect score, *then* I would forever be happy! I was so hyper-focused on the end result that I neglected the journey. Perhaps if had I tackled the disrespect which resulted in my misery, I could have avoided that vicious cycle. That's why I can tell you confidently that being a *lonely* hiker, a *jealous* hiker, and a *content* hiker is not the route to go. I've experienced all three at some point; the end result is long-term unhappiness.

When you're anything but a *persistent* hiker, you deceive yourself into believing that if you just had whatever it is that you desperately want, then having it will bring you happiness. That "thing," whatever it may be, eventually gets replaced with the "next thing." The vicious cycle thus continues. Don't buy into the lie.

My dad finally managed to kick his Nicotine addiction after 30 years. It was no easy feat. My dad's obsession started early on in his life. In the same way, it concerns me how many high schoolers are addicted to nicotine. "I only do it once or twice a day," many teen addicts might say. The craved buzz eventually wears out its novelty; it is no longer "good enough" anymore, claim researchers of Johns Hopkins Bloomberg School of Public Health. These researchers found that for all age groups combined, all of the 65.8% of participants who had ever smoked were: seven times more likely to have tried marijuana, seven times more likely to have tried cocaine, 14 times more likely to have tried crack, and 16 times more likely to have tried heroin.

Staggering, but why is that? As people tire of nicotine, they seek further pleasure in more "intense" drugs. These drugs, however, never satisfy them, leaving them altogether unhappy. As they search for the intensity which their first high gave them, they typically get more and more dependent. Eventually, in many cases, the original "experimenter" is unable to function while sober.

As Morrie lies on his deathbed, he notices that many of his visitors exude sorrow. He questions, "Why am I happy, and they are not?" Throughout his life, Morrie fled from the typical cultural founded upon success. Instead, his life became about loving and giving to others - especially his students. Now, even as his body is "losing connection" to itself, Morrie is having the time of his life. He figures out that love and human relationships result in the highest sense of worldly fulfillment.

The journey to the peak can become lonely, cumbersome, and can even feel meaningless at times - that is a promise. However, surges of energy come with helping others along their journey. According to a Mental Floss Article, this reenergizing act can be made as simple as volunteering a few hours each month. The article cited a study by a team of sociologists that monitored 2000 people over five years. They found that those who claimed they were "fulfilled" volunteered at least 5.8 hours each month. In a Psychology Today article, Marianna Pogosyan, Ph.D., cited a Columbia University study that even suggests that the person who helps someone reaps more benefits than the person that is helped. In the study, participants were linked to an anonymous online community where they could share stories of personally stressful situations. The participants were also able to provide support to the other participants. I almost couldn't believe the results of the study.

> "...helping others to regulate their emotions predicted better emotional and cognitive outcomes for those participants who were providing help. Moreover, because heightened levels of self-focused attention are common in depression, the more people helped others, the more their helping behavior predicted a reduction in their own depression, thanks to the use of reappraisal in their own daily lives... Interestingly, messages that used other-focused language (e.g., second-person pronouns such as you and your) were considered more helpful and garnered more gratitude from participants. In fact, using other-focused language not only helped the people in need, but also those who were helping."

Getting to the top of the mountain isn't all about just focusing on ourselves. One can argue, how can helping others benefit us? After all, how can we have time to get everything done in our day if we are focused on others? Focusing on others gives you more energy! Various studies have shown how focusing on others eliminates negative thoughts, ruminations, expectations, and fears that you have about your situation. That's worth repeating.

Study after study has shown how focusing on others eliminates negative thoughts, ruminations, expectations, and fears that you have about your situation.

As it is, helping others creates a domino effect. The more people you assist, the more the impact, the more people trust you. Then, when your time of need comes, people will be happy to help you! This, in turn, gives you more energy, productivity, and time to do what you set out to do. Let's not forget, on the journey you're about to set foot on, you will need as much help as you can get. By helping others, you will end up receiving more than you could have ever asked for. Soon, your service will have a ripple effect.

Remember Your Fallen Heroes

She was a class act, sharp as a tack, well-kempt, and my hero. She was a tiny soul weighing under ninety pounds. Even at the ripe old age of 70, she always looked the part; hair nicely groomed and modestly dressed as if preparing to attend church service. Old enough to be my grandmother, Mrs. McLean patiently and lovingly taught me to play the piano, starting from the age of five. A friend and neighbor gladly referred her as my parents searched the area for someone nearby.

Her modest home was always tidy, orderly, and clutter-free with the occasional knick-knack that usually represented a special memory of her deceased beloved spouse. Her house smelled either of freshly baked cookies or potpourri. It wasn't uncommon that after a lesson, she'd send her students home with a goodie bag of some sort. (I'd like to think that was just something she did for me, but I remember other kids leaving her house with a similar goodie bag in tow). Mrs. McLean was my piano teacher, but I grew to love her like my grandmother.

She was widowed long before she took me on as her student. She rarely discussed the late Mr. McClean, but I did remember overhearing her describe his last few years on this earth. What a small world I thought as I overheard my mother put two and two together when she discovered that the late Mr. McClean was the long-time band director at her old high school. I could tell there was an instant connection.

"Alright now, let's take it from the top, Skyler," I remember her saying to me. At the same time, we collaborated our chords to sound pleasing to the ear as she accompanied me on the piano. She would gently correct me as she motivated me with stickers and animated smiley faces after each perfected piece. She was a gentle soul and so loving about it - I wasn't always accustomed to that style of teaching, but I knew that I was drawn to it and that I looked forward to her lessons each week. "Shall we try it again or take a short break for some theory?" She'd cleverly say and do everything she could to sneak in that dreaded yet necessary music theory. How did she always manage to get me to do that? If that were anyone else, I would have objected - I hated music theory with a passion, but somehow we squeezed it in at almost every lesson - she was ingenious with her approach.

I often wonder why people weave in and out of our lives. Is it purposeful or by chance? Mrs. McClean was the constant encouragement in my life. With all my quirks and character flaws, she only saw potential and genius. She encouraged me in ways that nobody else did. I suppose that's why I looked forward to our lessons each week.

"Can I shovel your driveway, Mrs. McClean?" I'd holler as I'd walk by her house.

"Oh my, thank you, Skyler, but I have a service coming later today to do all that; would you like to come in for tea and cookies instead?" I couldn't say no, and three hours later, my phone was ringing off the hook with my worried mother asking me where I was.

Mrs. McClean was my mentor for over five years. The day she died left an indescribable hole in my heart. Hers was the first wake I had ever been to. As people made their way to pay their last respects, I patiently waited with anticipation - I just wanted one last time to talk to her and put closure on our relationship. I finally made my way over to her casket - she was beautifully dressed with makeup done just so. "Mrs. McClean, this is the piece I'm learning right now," I softly whispered in her ear as I showed her my music. I nervously fumbled through the pages in hopes that she could see and hear me. The tears started to flow from my eyes as I flipped through the sheet music. I blocked out everyone else around me. It was just the late Mrs. McClean and me. I thought about the many years we had together and the many duets we played. I reminisced about our tea and cookie visits oblivious to the time. I thought about the moment she lovingly told me it was time for me to move onto another teacher that could take me to another level.

"Are you Skyler Chauff - the Skyler Chauff?" I heard from distant voice, "Mom talked about you all the time - you were one of her favorite students!" she exclaimed.

What? How could that be? Though I smiled on the inside, I was heartbroken. Mrs. McClean was one of the few authority figures in my life who was a constant encouragement. I think of her often and fondly. She taught me that there was something to be said about a loving, gentle, and unconditional spirit. Stern discipline is characteristic in a structured environment, such as a military academy. Still, this petite, gray-haired woman taught me that sternness coupled with and or backed by love, produces powerful change. Though gone, her memory lives in my mind and heart forever. We all need a Mrs. McLean in our lives. I will forever be different because of her spirit.

FOURTEEN-BALANCE

"Balance suggests a perfect equilibrium. There is no such thing. That is a false expectation.... There are going to be priorities and dimensions of your life; how you integrate them is how you find true happiness." - Denise Morrison

You may be questioning whether *persistent* hikers truly exist. The answer is yes! This unique group has discovered the beauty of balance. My experiences, blunders, failures, and successes in and out of military school have shown me that the answer to the equation of success and happiness is **balance**. Not *my* version of balance. Not your parent's version of balance. Not your coach's version of balance. The type of balance that works within *your* life. The kind of balance that keeps you on *your* path.

Balance, when integrated properly, can be beneficial and extremely rewarding! Sure, it is super important to be motivated and want to fulfill your calling, to be focused on that goal, and to stick to that meticulously laid out schedule you may have made for yourself. All of those things are great tools to harness your productivity to be the best version of you.

Press on and keep going. However, take caution not to isolate yourself from the rest of the world. Bear in mind your friends, your family, and your support in the name of "success."

Remember the outcome of the lonely hiker.

When considering all my "moments" of highs and lows - lessons learned and doses of humble pie - I noticed that the majority of my struggles were the result of an imbalance in my life. Thomas Kinkade sums it up oh so nicely when he states that, "balance, peace, and joy are the fruit of a successful life. It starts with recognizing your talents and finding ways to serve others by using them." Isn't balance something we have control over? Yes, indeed, it is.

> *"We can be sure that the greatest hope for maintaining equilibrium in the face of any situation rests within ourselves." - Francis J. Braceland*

This isn't some obtuse, out of reach, improbable, pie in the sky undertaking - this balance is within your reach. You and I are the product of the choices we make. We can choose to have balance - that's great news! When I decided to mock authority, my phone was taken away, and I was forced to do lunges outside. I thought too much of myself and was, therefore, unable to meet new people under the guise of "shyness." I had cathexis for my girlfriend coupled with a poor self-image, and the relationship ended poorly. I wanted so desperately to be successful, and I worked myself to sickness. I craved perfection, and I wasted energy as a "correctional officer." I felt terrible about myself, and I projected my failures through gossiping about others. These were choices I made. The list continues beyond the scope of this book.

If my shortcomings, embarrassing moments, all-nighters, and military school training taught me anything, it is that a hardworking, purposeful, and balanced life leads to long-lasting success and happiness. Balance also includes coming to terms with something that many world-renowned scientists, CEOs, physicists, and philosophers have concluded: we are being guided by a force much more powerful than ourselves. This force, whether you acknowledge it as God, a higher power, or Karma, is continuously at work in our lives.

This force might also determine what your point B might be. Remember, you are a hiker on a path to ***point B***: an oasis or the top of the mountain where you find your dream job, house, vacation, spouse, or whatever you envision for your dream life to be. So what if your path includes rugged terrain or you stumble into a cave. Make decisions that will enhance your journey, not prolong it. Remember that gossiping and slandering, unnecessary all-nighters, partying, and negative thinking are mainly activities that fill the lives of lost hikers who are stagnant or still stuck at base camp.

Think 20 years into the future, when you are interviewing to get that dream job. Maybe just one year in the future, when you are up for that employee evaluation, college acceptance, or that big promotion. Remember, you'll be competing with others on a similar journey. In contrast, there will also be hikers who have partied, "enjoyed" life to the fullest, and spent their lives chasing false dreams. Ultimately, the hiker who stayed on that straight and narrow path is more likely to have a better resume, the sophistication, and the experience to be qualified for the job. Stay on your track and navigate your caves even when the journey becomes tiresome with no end in sight.

For all of the socially awkward, misbehaving, lonely, lost, and unaccepted people out there, I have stood in your shoes. I am still socially inept, I sometimes feel alone, and I even veer off of my journey at times. I have felt your pain in my awkward, embarrassing, and unfortunate experiences. However, scars from my mistakes keep me determined and on my journey.

Refrain from spending too much of your time surrounded by those who put down on you and others, gossip, and waste time complaining - they aren't necessarily looking for a solution but rather a sounding board. This repeated pattern can suck you into a vortex of emotional garbage. Stop allowing others to dictate your path! Instead, entrust yourself to those whose counsel has your best interest at heart. Get on the road of the persistent hiker and carry on.

Always remember that nothing extraordinary is attainable without intense training and work. Accept that YOU WILL SUFFER. The perfect relationship may come after several losses, harsh breakups, and broken hearts. Good grades come as a result of hard work, sacrificing time, and dedication to learning. Mental and physical fitness is achieved at the price of enduring pain. In the end, persevering through the treacherous and difficult path toward the summit is the only way to attain real success, happiness, and peace.

"So, what did you do to get a letter of assurance from the United States Military Academy?" Someone recently asked me. It reminded me of the question asked of me years ago. That life-changing question which inspired and prompted me to write this book at the ripe old age of 15 "So what did you do to end up in a military school?"

When confronted with that question, I didn't quite know how to respond. I also knew better than to tell my mother. I envisioned her marching over to my friend's house and giving his mom a piece of her mind. It wasn't until a year after the fact that I finally told her my plans to write a book. Surprised and ambivalent, my mother asked what prompted me to do so. As I proceeded to share the series of events that led up to it, I could see an unfamiliar look in her eyes; I didn't know how to interpret it. "Mom, it's ok, I'm not angry, it just motivates me all the more to get my version out," I assured her.

She was tearful but with tears of pride. "Good for you, son." She managed to get out.

What I did to get a letter of assurance from West Point? In a nutshell, I accomplished roughly 14,064 pushups, 540 room inspections, 1023 accountability formations, 18 marching parades, 5,000 hours of studying, 1,000 community service hours, six leadership positions, 400 miles of running, four summers of leadership training, two failed relationships, read 36 self-help books, and ate roughly 126 doses of humble pie.

THIS is my story, and this is my path.

FIFTEEN-THIS IS THEIR STORY, THIS IS THEIR PATH

So what happened to the other characters? I'll tell you what I know about their paths. Zhang is currently working on getting his pilot's license. From what I hear, he is an awesome pilot. Kevin Moon is getting a degree in education at the University of Wisconsin-Madison. He now has a youtube channel that is growing in popularity. Tommy ended up going to another military academy before moving back to Texas and to finish his last year in high school. Porter is in his last year with me at St. John's. We still reminisce about old times together. Geo was accepted into the University of Illinois Urbana - Champaign. However, he just completed basic training. He was recently offered a contract to try out for special forces. Having completed basic training, Geo is at Urbana-Champaign and is applying for West Point. Adar is a platoon leader at St. John's. During the first quarter, his platoon overall scored the highest in GPA, community service, PT scores, and inspection scores. He was recently promoted and, while I'm writing this, has above a 4.0 GPA.

CSM Jim attends St. Norbert College and has completed two

140-mile hikes to raise awareness for veteran suicide. William is at the University of North Dakota looking to soon become a pilot. Sergeant John Chris is on his way to becoming a 2nd Lieutenant after he completes two more years at the United States Military Academy. I still call him for advice on running the Corps of Cadets as well as he did. Squad Leader Din is studying at Purdue University and will be applying to medical schools next year. Jabin Victor is attaining a degree in biology at Loyola University. His newest set of advice is to "study a week-and-a-half before any college test." Charlie Robby is studying at the University of Louisville. He still calls me and yells, "Stop studying, Skyler!!" Finally, yes, I get along much better with the night guards.

ACKNOWLEDGE-MENTS

First and foremost, I want to thank the parent who gave me the inspiration to share my story. With all due respect, your confrontation inspired me to write this book. I have no ill will toward you - for I too was misinformed about military schools.

    I also want to thank everyone who helped me conquer my caves. Michael and Liam, thank you for always being there for me, even during my less than glorious days. Yes, you both are the hardest working staff members. Michael, you inspire me to work harder every single day. Liam, I wouldn't be where I'm at without our friendship. Tolebi, I wouldn't be where I'm at today without your support. Please know that I wouldn't have wanted anyone else by my side during such a hard time. I wish I could have been there for you more. Kelvin, you inspire me to be the best version of myself. Hongbo, I've never had a friend quite like you that I could always run with, study with, and watch movies with on the weekends. Jorjito, keep smiling because you're going to be something amazing some day. Let me know when I can submit my resume to you for a job.

Parker, without a doubt, you are the smartest person I've ever met. Someone with your smarts could change the world. Junsu, there's a purpose in this world for your computer skills - the tutoring was just the beginning. Anders, you're the definition of discipline. You've challenged me here from day one. Without you to look up to, I can't say that I would have made it this far. Sean Bornschlegl, thank you for the golf course talks and the "interventions." Max Johnson, Andrew Burrow, Jacob Kelley, Matthew Moore, and Chris Slosar, you inspired me to be more than I ever thought I could be. Thank you.

Mom, without you, this book would have never happened. You spent hours helping me correct my less than perfect grammar and my unorganized ideas. Thank you for beating this stubborn mule into submission; I wouldn't be where I'm at today if it weren't for your patience and persistence. Dad, thank you for always supporting me, making me laugh, and for being such an amazing role model. Thank you Jay for showing me unconditional love. You're such an amazing brother. My leadership is a reflection of your character. Papou, thank you for babysitting me when I was four years old. Thank you for running after me as I ran circles around you, building legos with me, and for spending hours teaching me Greek. Your fighting mentality motivated me to finish this book in time for you to be able to read it. Yaya, thank you for always making me the best pancakes ever! Mrs. McClean, you will always hold a special place in my heart - I miss you big time.

Thea Rubina, Theo Perry, Peter, and Alex, I want to thank you for your constant support. Thank you for always making Christmas such an awesome time. For the many trips to Lai Tai, thank you, Theo Harry and Thea Joanne.

Thank you to all my friends back home. Thank you Tim, Luke, Kameron, Sean, Sean, Jackson, Brett, Niko, Casey, Jimmy, John, and the rest of the gang. Thank you for keeping me in the loop on plans even though I was miles away - you guys always included me.

To my coach Yevgeny, thank you for your tough love and

for never letting up. To Master David, thank you for taking me under your wing.

To my mentors Mr. Jonathan and Mrs. Melody, thank you for your many hours of tutoring and believing in me.

Thank you Mr. Erickson, Mr. Bennett, Tom Stocks, Dr. Albert, Dr. Wozniac, Major Mayer, Colonel Kebisek, Sergeant Trione, General Lima, First Sergeant David, Aunt Eileen, Mr. Muse, Mr. Stadler, Dr. Lee, Sergeant Spreitzer, Mr. Lavictor, Chief Schweiss, Dr. Roehrkasse, Dr. Henery, Mrs. Sebo, First Sergeant Zimmer, Sergeant Frame, Sergeant Anderson, Mrs. Staffeldt, Mrs. Mauer, Mrs. Collins, Master David, Mrs. Sebo, and Marlee for going above and beyond to inspire, mentor and put up with me. I thank you from the bottom of my heart.

Thank you leadership and members of the 136th Corps of Cadets and to St. John's Northwestern Military Academy. You have truly impacted my life forever.

Finally, I thank God for giving me the drive, guidance, and heart to write this book.

◆ ◆ ◆

Works Cited

Chapter 2 - 911, What Is Your Emegency
1. Klein, Alyson. "No Child Left Behind Overview: An Overview." Education Week, 10 Apr. 2015, www.edweek.org/ew/section/multimedia/no-child-left-behind-overview-definition-summ
Ary.html.

Chapter 5 - Baby Steps
1. Hardy, Darren. *The Compound Effect: Jumpstart Your Income, Your Life, Your Success*. Vanguard Press, 2010.

2. Nguyen, Hoang. "A Third of Americans Habitually Make Their Beds." YouGov, 23 Jan. 2018, today.yougov.com/topics/lifestyle/articles-reports/2018/01/23/third-americans-habitually-

make-their-beds.

3. Sáez, Francisco. "Micro-Tasks. The Pleasure of Checking Off." FacileThings - Your Life, Simple, https://facilethings.com/blog/en/micro-tasks.

4. Selk, Jason and Tom Bartow. *Organize Tomorrow Today: 8 Ways to Retrain Your Mind to Optimize Performance at Work and in Life.* Da Capo, 2016.

Chapter 6 - Breakthrough

1. Chaudhary, Kulreet. "Sleep and Longevity." *Doctoroz.com*, 2019, www.doctoroz.com/blog/kulreet-chaudhary-md/sleep-and-longevity.

2. "Get Enough Sleep." *Healthfinder.gov*, U.S. Department of Health and Human Services, 2019, healthfinder.gov/healthtopics/category/everyday-healthy-living/mental-health-and-relatio nship/get-enough-sleep#the-basics_2.

3. The Healthline Editorial Team and Rachel Nall. "The Science of Sleep: Why You Need 7 to 8 Hours a Night." *Healthline*, Healthline Media, 27 Mar. 2019, www.healthline.com/health/science-sleep-why-you-need-7-8-hours-night#live-longer.

4. Tyley, Jodie. "What Happens to Your Body When You Sleep?" *The Independent*, Independent. Digital News and Media, 1 Oct. 2015, www.independent.co.uk/life-style/health-and-families/features/what-happens-to-your-body-when-you-sleep-a6675861.html.

Chapter 7 - Nobody Cares About You, Forget Your Ego

1. "11 Facts About Global Poverty." *DoSomething.org*, www.dosomething.org/us/facts/11-facts-about-global-poverty.

2. Burchard, Brendon. *High Performance Habits: How Extraordinary People Become That Way.* Hay House, Inc., 2017.

3. Lakhiani, Vishen. *The Code of the Extraordinary Mind: 10 Laws to Enhance Happiness, Mindfulness, and Influence.* Simon & Schuster, 2016.

Chapter 8 - Be Like a Child

1. Dickson, John. *Humilitas: A Lost Key to Life, Love, and Leadership.* Zondervan, 2011.

2. Eisenberg, Dana. "15 Inspirational Rags - To - Riches Stories." Business Insider, Business Insider, 28 Dec. 2011, www.businessinsider.com/rags-to-riches-stories-2011-11#sheldon-adelson-is-another-

las-vegas-hotels-magnate-who-tried-his-hand-at-a-few-industries-9.

3. Gale, James. "British People Spend over Six Hours a Week Feeling Guilty." The Independent, Independent Digital News and Media, 2 Feb. 2018, www.independent.co.uk/life-style/guilt-british-six-hours-week-feeling-a8190896.html.

4. Peck, M. Scott. *The Road Less Traveled, A New Psychology of Love, Traditional Values, and Spiritual Growth.* Simon and Schuster, 1978.

5. Schamblin, Gwen. *History Of The One True God: The Origin of Good and Evil.* Vol. 2, Remnant Publishing, 2017.

6. Strobel, Lee, and Jane Vogel. *The Case for a Creator: a Journalist Investigates Scientific Evidence That Points Toward God.* Zondervan, 2014.

Chapter 10 - Finding One's Calling

1. DoSomething.org Editors. "11 Facts About High School Dropout Rates." DoSomething.org, www.dosomething.org/us/facts/11-facts-about-high-school-dropout-rates.

2. Dunn, Alan. "Average America vs the One Percent." Forbes, Forbes Magazine, 26 July 2012, www.forbes.com/sites/moneywisewomen/2012/03/21/average-america-vs-the-one-percent/.

3. Gladwell, Malcolm. *Outliers: the Story of Success.* Back Bay Books, 2013.

4. Peters, Ralph. "TROOPS & CRIMES." New York Post, New York Post Holdings, Inc., 3 Aug. 2007, nypost.com/2007/08/03/troops-crimes/.

5. Ramos, Yuritzy. "College Students Tend to Change Majors When They Find the One They Really Love." Borderzine, Borderzine, 15 Mar. 2013, borderzine.com/2013/03/college-students-tend-to-change-majors-when-they-find-the-one-they-really-love/.

Chapter 11 - Adolf Chauff, Yes Mr. Correctional Officer

1. Mcleod, Saul. "The Stanford Prison Experiment." Stanford Prison Experiment | Simply Psychology, 1 Jan. 1970, www.simplypsychology.org/zimbardo.html.

Chapter 12 - It's the Journey, Not the Destination

1. Goggins, David. *Cant Hurt Me: Master Your Mind and Defy the Odds.* Lioncrest Publishing, 2018.

Chapter 13 - The Meaning in Relationships

1. Albom, Mitch. *Tuesdays with Morrie: An Old Man, a Young Man, and Life's Greatest Lesson*. Broadway Books, 2017.

2. Cigarette Smoking Gateway to Illegal Drug Use. Johns Hopkins Bloomberg School of Public Health, 6 Dec. 2000, www.jhsph.edu/news/news-releases/2000/smoking-drugs.html.

3. "7 Scientific Benefits of Helping Others." Mental Floss, 4 Dec. 2015, mentalfloss.com/article/71964/7-scientific-benefits-helping-others.

4. Pogosyan, Marianna. "In Helping Others, You Help Yourself." Psychology Today, Sussex Publishers, 30 May 2018, www.psychologytoday.com/us/blog/between-cultures/201805/in-helping-others-you-help-yourself.

Made in the USA
Lexington, KY
09 December 2019